TH

C000022834

THE RUNES
AND OTHER MAGICAL ALPHABETS

by
Michael Howard

THE AQUARIAN PRESS LIMITED
Wellingborough, Northamptonshire

First published 1978
First paperback Edition 1981
Second Impression 1983
Third Impression 1984
Fourth Impression 1987

British Library Cataloguing in Publication Data

Howard, Michael, *b. 1948*
    The runes and other magical alphabets.
    1. Runes
    I. Title
    417'.7   PD2013

    ISBN 0-85030-244-7

Printed and bound in Great Britain

'A man is insane who writes a secret in any way other than one which will conceal it from the vulgar.'

Roger Bacon

To Rosina

CONTENTS

ACKNOWLEDGEMENTS

The publisher would like to thank the following for permission to reproduce the photographs in this book.

Radio Times Hulton Picture Library
'Odin, northern god of war'.
Roman tessellated pavement with swastika design.
Hitler's May Day speech, 1939.
Hitler's SS bodyguard.
Dr John Dee.
Aleister Crowley.

The British Museum
The Rosetta Stone.
Panel of the Franks casket.
Jutish sword carved with runes.

The Manx Museum
Thorwald's cross-slab.

Mr Kenneth Grant
Austin Osman Spare.

Department of the Environment
The Ruthwell Cross.

1.

THE MAGIC OF WRITING

Writing, as any school-child will tell you, is a means of communication using letters formed to create words and is in essence 'materialized language'. An alphabet can be defined as a set of letters used in language or writing and is derived from the first two words of the Greek system of writing – alpha and beta. The subject of this book is *magical* alphabets which suggests something apart, distinctive from everyday use and possibly surrounded by some supranormal awe. Yet the idea has its origins in the cave paintings of ancient man who could see no distinction between magic and the normal routine of life. In fact, without recourse to magic early man believed that there could be no survival of the harsh rigours of life in his primitive environment. While we today may laugh at his fears and ridicule him for his superstitious viewpoint, he was correct within the limits of his own consciousness, for without the discipline of magical ritual the structure of Stone Age society would have collapsed.

If we examine the ancient paintings found in the cave homes of our early ancestors we can perceive the attempts, by developing humanity to express ideas in symbols, to communicate ideas and to translate them into a magical code easily understood by other members of the tribe apart from the cave artist. Many of these symbols had a magico-religious meaning and the symbolic drawing of a strong warrior chasing and killing a deer was easily understood by the tribe.

Enacted as a hunting fertility rite by the stag-masked

shaman it became a living symbol glyph for the tribe to concentrate on and understand. Intercommunication between different minds by word pictures had been born in the Stygian darkness of the caves where early man was taught the rudiments of mental contact.

From this early beginning developed the first true writing forms and the first of these was the cuneiform script used by the nomadic tribes of the Near East. These people settled the fertile valleys of Mesopotamia and eventually created a great civilization from a deserted and lonely wilderness. As its Latin name suggests, cuneiform was a wedge-shaped script and is regarded by experts as the first identifiable form of writing. It originated in early picture writing and many of the myths, magical formulae and demonic invocations used by the Assyrian, Babylonian and Chaldean astrologers and priest-magicians were carved in cuneiform on clay tablets. Hundreds of these have been excavated by archaeologists from ancient sites in the Near and Middle East and are now on display in Western museums and cultural centres.

Picture writing received a new impetus in the dynasties of the Ancient Egyptian pharaohs when hieroglyphics (*hiero* sacred, *glyph* carving) were devised by the priesthood to conceal their magical secrets. In this system material objects served as symbols for words or phrases, i.e. the word *ibis* was represented by an actual drawing of the bird. It would seem that the Egyptian priests regarded the art of writing as such an important art that they even claimed that its secrets were imparted to them by the ibis-headed god, Thoth or Tehuti.

This concept that writing was a gift from the gods was not confined to the Egyptian priests and is echoed in the myths and legends of many other ancient civilizations. In Babylon the god Nebo was regarded as the author of cuneiform, Hermes invented the Greek alphabet, Moses was given the Hebrew script on the mountain top and in Western Europe it was the all-father, Odin, who passed the mysteries of the written word to his human children.

Enoch's Vision
The tradition mentioned above that Moses was given the

Hebrew alphabet from a divine source is a little-known story and worth expanding upon for it throws new light on the esoteric lore of the Jewish race. Justification for the claim can be found in the apocryphal text called *The Book Of Enoch*. In this ancient codex the Old Testament prophet, Enoch, has a vision of heaven and its angelic inhabitants and one of these is Metraton, the archangel of the Presence (of God). The archangel says to Enoch '... come and behold the letters by which Heaven and Earth were created, the letters by which were created mountains and hills, the letters by which were created rivers and seas, the letters by which were created the trees and the herbs.'

Enoch was naturally impressed by these revelations but more sensational news was to come, for Metraton turned once more to the prophet and spoke saying

> The God of Israel is my witness that when I revealed this secret to Moses, then all the Hosts of Heaven raged against me saying 'Why dost thou reveal this secret to Moses, to a son of man, born of woman, tainted and unclean? The secret by which was created land and sea, ... the Garden of Eden, the Tree of Life, by which were formed Adam and Eve, the cattle and wild beasts, the fowl of the air and the fish of the sea, the creeping things and the Tora of Wisdom, knowledge and thought and the Gnosis of things above. Why dost thou reveal this to flesh and blood O Mighty Metraton?'

This myth agrees with an occult tradition that the clay tablets of the ten commandments were mundane laws suited to the control of the base instincts of the unruly Hebrew tribes, who had already proved themselves unworthy of the truly sacred laws by their heretical worship and adoration of the golden bull idol. The original sacred laws, according to occult lore, were engraved on emerald tablets which Moses destroyed when he discovered the orgiastic rites which the children of Israel were indulging in around the effigy of a horned god.

Hieratic Symbols
Returning once more to the hieroglyphs of Egypt, we find that the teaching of this magical form of picture writing was

The Rosetta Stone.

reserved for the priests and the sons of royalty and nobility, who were automatically initiated into the magico-religious rites at an early age. The priesthood used the hieroglyph system to conceal the mysteries of the Egyptian religion from the ordinary people and, while some of the more elementary picture symbols were in common parlance, the majority – termed *hieratic* symbols – were known and used only by initiates of the temples. This was the beginning of the true magical alphabets, as esoteric codes used to hide secret knowledge or teachings from the masses, and their purpose has changed little in the intervening centuries up to the present day, despite the major changes and technical developments in techniques of communication.

It is, in fact, a lasting tribute to the genius of the Egyptian masters of magic that their mystical alphabet remained undeciphered until the last century. The breakthrough came as late as 1822, when a Frenchman called Jean Champollian revealed the secrets of the famous Rosetta Stone. This was a black basalt slab covered in hieroglyphics, which had been dug up by French soldiers excavating trenches in 1799, and it gave details of a royal decree issued under the authority of Ptolemy Pharaoh V in 197 BC. Its inscription was written in both hieratic and demotic – or proletariat – scripts, with a translation in the conventional Greek alphabet underneath.

Champollian worked for fourteen years on the stone before it gave up its secrets and he managed to complete the work commenced some years before by other Egyptian scholars. The actual turning point in his research came when he recognized Ptolemy's name enclosed in a *cartouche*, or oval frame, which was an honour only bestowed on the names or titles of very important Egyptian persons. The Frenchman successfully interpreted the hieroglyphs making up the Pharaoh's name and used this as a key word to translate the rest of the stone. For the first time in many thousands of years the magical alphabet of the Ancient Egyptian priest-magicians was once more read and understood.

Ogham Alphabet
Moving westward from the classical landscapes of the Near

and Middle East, we find that forms of writing had also been
developed by the Celtic tribes, who had settled the lowlands of
Western Europe and had conquered both the British Isles and
Ireland. One of the most famous magical alphabets used by
the Celts was *ogham*, a system of writing taking its name from
the Celtic sun god, Ogha, who was said to be its inventor.
While this is the popular belief, the historical version of
ogham's origin is that it first appeared in the Celtic
settlements of the west coast of Ireland and was derived from
the finger language employed by the Druids or 'priests of the
oak tree'.

Ogham was regarded as a magical alphabet because it was
reputed to have been used by the Celtic gods and heroes and
there are several references to it in mythology. In one of the
tales relating to the Irish hero Cu Chulainn it is said,

> He went in to a wood and cut an oak sapling with one stroke,
> standing on one leg and using one eye. He twisted it to a ring and
> carved an Ogham inscription on it. This ring he placed on the
> standing stone at Ard Cuillen and forced it down till it touched
> the thickest part of the stone. The nobles of Ireland came to the
> stone and saw the ring and Ailill gave the ring to Fergus who told
> the men of Ireland what the inscription said. When he had
> finished he said, 'This is a ring. What is its meaning to us? What
> is its secret message? Who put it here? Was it one man or many?'
> And none could tell him.

Cu Chullainn was also said to have been skilled in a secret
language known as *berla na filied* which may have been a
variation on ogham or some other magical writing. Oral
sorcery was certainly recognized as a skill unique to the Celtic
Druids and bards and was remarked upon by their opponents
and enemies. Roman travellers often commented on the Celts
love of words and mastery of language. Diodorus Siculus said
of the Gaulish priests he had encountered, 'In conversation
they use very few words but they speak in riddles for the most
part, hinting at things and leaving a great deal to be
understood.'

Ogham itself is an alphabet of five groups of five letters,
represented by one to five lines extending away from a
horizontal line. In the first group the lines extend above the

horizontal and in the second below it. In the third perpendicular above and below, in the fourth diagonally and in the fifth the lines are heterogeneous. It is a simple but effective system of writing using the basic straight line as the ruling pattern.

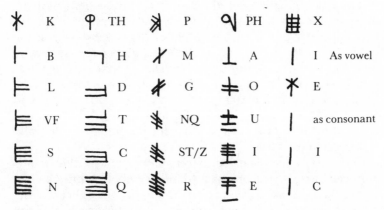

The Celtic Ogham script.

As well as its use by the Celtic heroes and the Druids, ogham was also employed by ordinary people for magical purposes. It was used as a magical alphabet carved on talismans and amulets and there is an amber bead in the British Museum which has inscribed on it an ogham phrase to protect the wearer from the dangers inherent in childbirth. The use of amber in this way was quite common in ancient times and in AD 588 clerical leaders preached sermons against the wearing of amber amulets saying, 'Let no woman hang amber around her neck or have recourse to enchanters or engravers of amber.'

The Tree Alphabet
A second Celtic alphabet existed which was even more magically potent and secret than ogham and this was the *beth luis nion* or *tree alphabet*. As its name suggests, it was based on the magico-religious significance of trees which acted as

symbols for words and letters. Part of its occult lore was based upon the cycle of seasonal rites, associated with plant, tree and animal growth, practised by the Celts. It was a secret code that was easily passed to the Druid initiates because its mysteries were found all around, in the forests which covered most of the British islands on those days.

The tree alphabet was divided into four sections and the most important were the seven major letters, or *chieftains*, which were symbolized by the following trees – oak, hazel, holly, yew, ash, pine and apple. At first glance the latter may seem the odd tree out, until you remember that it played host to the white berries of the mistletoe, which was sacred to the Druid rites of midwinter. The apple was also regarded in Celtic times as the food of the gods and Avalon – the kingdom of the dead in Welsh myth and Arthurian romance – literally translated means 'the sacred place of the apples'.

Oak trees were regarded as very important by the Druids who venerated the acorn as a phallic symbol. A little known fact is that the word *glans*, referring to the conical head of the male sex organ, is derived from the Latin for acorn, and the resemblance between the two objects is quite pronounced. Hazel branches have traditionally given birth to the magician's wand and the witch's broomstick, the red berries of the holly symbolized the spilt blood of the sacrificed god or 'divine king'. The yew tree is associated in English folklore with death, while the ash represents new life and the pine cone is another symbol of the phallus in Celtic myths.

In the second category of sacred trees were the alder, sacred to the magician-god Bran the Blessèd, the willow, usually associated in Celtic legends with the moon goddess Ceridwen, and the hawthorn or faery tree. In addition to these we also find rowan, which protected mortals from dark magic, the birch tree, used for flagellation rites, and the elm, which was another tree with connotations of death.

The third and fourth sections of the tree alphabet included blackthorn, elder, poplar, ivy, broom, furze and several others, giving twenty-nine letters in total. Each had its attendant religious mysteries and magical rites which were only revealed to the Druidic initiates. As the probationary period for entry to the priesthood was twenty years of rigorous training, by the time the initiate received the secrets of the *beth luis nion* it was very unlikely that he would willingly reveal its mysteries to any outsider.

Irish Druids seem to have been the strictest taught, for their apprenticeship to the magical craft was both hard and very long. Their priests were divided into different classes or ranks which included the *fili* or poet-seers. This caste of priest was authorized to practise divination – which sometimes included the evisceration of small animals to find signs and omens in the entrails – and taught to read, write and decipher the Celtic magical alphabets. It took a fili twelve years to learn his craft and many more years to perfect the art to the high standard expected by the elder Druids.

The training was largely oral and consisted of the Chief Druid intoning poetic verses, recounting myths and retelling the exploits of famous heroes, while the pupil strove to commit it all to memory. Once trained, the fili often took the role of travelling bard, wandering up and down the country composing ballads and reciting poetry. As a nomadic holy man he was always sure of a warm welcome, a good meal and a soft bed, as few Celtic chieftains would gamble on upsetting the gods by harming a Druid or refusing him food and shelter.

The Mouth of the Oak

Each letter of the tree alphabet also represented a monthly period in the Celtic calendar and, during that time, in a sequence geared to the moon's phrases, the rites pertaining to the sacred tree ruling that month were performed. I will take two examples as illustrations of these magical rites – first the month of *Duir*, the oak, which runs from 10 June to 7 July and, secondly, the month of *Tinne* which follows it from 8 July to 4 August inclusive.

As we have seen, the oak is associated with the sun god, Ogha or Lugh, and his season is midsummer, when the power of the solar rays are at their strongest. The code phrase for this period is 'I am the God who sets the head afire with smoke' and Robert Graves, the poet and author, suggests in his classic work *The White Goddess* (Faber and Faber, 1948) that this refers to the narcotic qualities of the fumes produced by burning oak leaves.

Midsummer bonfires were festive occasions up until Christian times and, originally, it is conceivable that the presiding Druid scattered dried oak leaves over the flames. As the people leapt through the fire they inhaled the acrid smoke which, as well as causing headaches, dizzy spells and sore eyes, could have acted as an inspirational narcotic causing the afflicted to cry out in the 'tongues of the Gods'. Hallucinogenic drugs were well-known to the Druids and they certainly knew and used the natural psychedelic known as 'the sacred mushroom' – the red-capped *fly agaric* fungus.

Tinne was traditionally the month of sacrifice and in the Celtic myths it was explained by the esoteric phrase, 'I am a spear waging war'. It was during the month of *Tinne* that the human representative of the father god met his death by ritual spearing. He was called the *tanist*, according to Robert Graves, and the weapon used to despatch him from the earthy plane was the same shape as the modern capital letter T, depicted in later Celtic-Norse runes as a ↑ shape.

At the height of the summer the god had to die and the divine king's reign ended in death by ritual sacrifice. In the sky the sun waned in power from its zenith at the summer solstice and entered the ebbing tide moving towards the autumn equinox and the cold winter. 'As above, so below', the ritual pattern is worked to reflect the changing of the seasons and the cycle of solar rebirth.

In the mysteries of the magical tree alphabet, Graves tells us, the human representative of the god is made drunk with mead and is bound naked to a T-shaped oak cross. This cross stands behind a rough hewn stone altar, within a circle of twelve standing-stones – making the mystic thirteen, the number of moons in the old year. The divine victim is bound to the cross with willow thongs in the five-fold bond, which links wrists, neck and ankles, and is flagellated. As the rite reaches its climax, a spear made of mistletoe wood is thrust up and between the ribs of the victim and he dies screaming the name of the sacrificial god. It is believed that the sacrificer was usually a priestess, possibly a member of the female Druid cult, or a wisewoman of the older aboriginal religion discovered by the Celts when they crossed from the Continent and settled here.

Although this is a grim account of human sacrifice, bear in mind the victim usually volunteered to die and went to the sacrificial altar considering it an honour. Certainly not all the religious rites associated with the tree alphabet were such bloody ceremonies. Another summer festival was *Uath* in May which had rites of fertility, love, happiness and sexual liberation. In the ancient Celtic beliefs, May was considered an unlucky month and this probably accounts for the old English saying, 'Ne'er cast clout till May be out'. This supersition refers to not changing winter clothing for light summer wear till either the month is over or the blossom has bloomed on the May tree. In either case, the superstition dates from the cleansing and purification rites of the pagan temples in May and the preparations for the midsummer rites when new clothes were worn. It lingers on today in the annual ritual of 'spring cleaning' indulged in by modern housewives. Perhaps this is a subconscious racial memory of distant days when cleaning was an important religious rite.

The tree associated with *Uath* in the Celtic tree alphabet was hawthorn and this was also regarded as the sacred tree of the faeries. It was a very important tree to the Celts, as its flowers were connected symbolically with the worship of the white goddess, the patron deity of the British Isles. In the Middle Ages hawthorn branches were placed atop the phallic maypoles gracing every village green and the traditional 'slap and tickle' during the Mayday festivities is a sublimated relic of the pagan fertility rites to assist the growth of the spring vegetation.

Uath (13 May to 9 June) was therefore a time of love-making, wild festivity, laughter and joy – a last erotic fling before the bloodstained spectacle of the midsummer rites with their overtones of ritual slaughter to the old gods.

I mentioned earlier the significance of the letter T in the shape of the ritual weapon used at the solstice ceremony. This relates to the most famous, but still little understood or researched, magical alphabet known to ancient man – the

sacred writing of the *runes*. It is this potent, secret and sinister
script I will now examine, for it is the hiding place of a system
of neglected pagan magic and the precursor of our modern
alphabet.

2.

THE ORIGIN OF THE RUNES

The subject of the runes is shrouded in myth and mystery, clouded by deception and wrapped in secrecy and superstition. Scholars even disagree on the fundamental information of when and where runic writing first appeared in Europe. The consensus of opinion is that the runes developed out of the picture carvings and rock symbols called the Hallristingnor script. These carvings were executed by Neolithic and Bronze Age artists belonging to the Germanic tribes who settled in Northern Italy and parts of modern Austria and Germany. They depict *swastikas*, or sunwheels, strange angular sigils and other symbols sacred to the shaman magicians of the German tribes.

Archaeologists can still only speculate on the exact form the religious beliefs of early European man took but, from available evidence and surviving folk traditions, it is possible to say that the principle objects of worship were a horned god and a goddess, either in the form of the fertile earth mother or the enchanting moon goddess. These beliefs, in many different manifestations, were not only common to the Celtic tribes of Gaul, Britain and Ireland but were adapted and modified by the later Norse and Saxon races. They originated in Stone Age times and by the Iron Age were well established in Western Europe and the Scandinavian countries.

Religious objets d'art, excavated from Danish and Swedish

burial mounds of this period, depict the sun as a wheel (the runic swastika) harnessed to a sacred horse, the symbol of the goddess. The Nordic warriors carried on their battle helmets the twin horns of the god, symbolizing the rays of the rising sun in the dawn sky. Some rune experts have speculated that the three-legged seal of the Isle of Man, an island colonized by Norse seafarers, may be a crude representation of the swastika and a close relation of the sacred rune signs of the Teutonic tribes of Germany and Northern Italy. Alternatively it is claimed that the Manx sigil originates from Sicily and was brought from that island by the Normans who invaded Man in the Middle Ages.

The Hallristingnor rock carvings, the ancient script from which the runes were derived. Note the important magical sigils of the sun wheel, swastika and spiral.

Whispered Secrets

The word *rune* itself is derived from the Norse *runar*, magic sign, and the Old German *runa*, meaning either 'to whisper' or 'a secret'. The term to 'rown', 'roon' or 'round' in the ear was in common usage in Anglo-Saxon England and signified the whispering of a secret. This etymological connection with whispered secrets and the esoteric makes the runes not only an important method of recondite communication in writing but singles it out from other scripts as a truly magical alphabet, composed of word symbols believed to possess occult powers in the hands of a person skilled in their use and conversant with the inner meanings of each symbol.

Since the runes were categorized as a magical alphabet they had to boast a supernatural origin, so they were generally credited as an invention of the Norse god, Odin, known as Woden or Wotan in Germany and by the title Grim, the 'hooded one', in Anglo-Saxon England. The name Odin is derived either from the root words 'wind' or 'spirit' and he was a deity representing the wilder aspects of nature encountered in Northern climes. Odin was the god of the Scandinavian underworld, the dark forests of the Northlands, and ruler of the hosts of the dead and unborn. He features frequently in the Norse myths and is regarded as the all-father, the god who make the gods, the creator of the worlds of men, demons and shining ones.

In human form, Odin was pictured as a warrior, in armoured mail with shield, sword and spear at the ready to do battle, or as a travelling man. In the latter anthropormorphic disguise Odin could be encountered by any wayfarer on the open road and was described as a tall figure, wrapped in a long dark cloak, with a wide-brimmed hat or hood drawn down over the eye which was a gaping, empty socket. His hair was steel grey and cascaded down to his shoulders, while his one good eye was icy blue, shining with an unholy light which burned into the soul of anyone who crossed his path.

The rune god was accompanied on his travels by two ravens and two wolves who were his familiars. His horse, named Sleipnir, had eight legs. A famous rune riddle asks, 'Who has eight feet, one eye and two hands?' and the answer was Odin riding Sleipnir. When Christianity began to erode the old pagan beliefs, it was Odin or Woden who became the leading horseman in the dreaded 'wild hunt' which rode across the skies hunting the souls of the dead. In later times the name *Grim* was even literally translated by monks as 'devil' and the old Norse god was relegated to a position as yet another aspect

'Odin, northern god of war' by V.C. Prinsep.

of the mythical Satan believed in by good Christians.

Odin was also the patron god of magicians and so it is not really surprising that ordinary people regarded him as the inventor of the runes. Some students of the old religions see Odin as an European version of the Greek god, Hermes and the Egyptian deity of writing, Thoth, who was credited with discovering hieroglyphics. The link between Hermes, Thoth and Odin is illustrated by the following tenth century rhyme, obviously of Christian origin as it reflects cynicism and disbelief in the pagan gods.

> Once there lived a man,
> who was Mercury called,
> he was vastly deceitful
> and cunning in his deeds,
> he loved well to steal,
> and all lying tricks,
> the heathens had made him
> the highest of their gods,
> and at the crossroads
> they offered him booty,
> and to the high hills
> brought him victims to slay,
> this god was most honoured
> among all the heathens,
> his name when translated
> to Danish is Odin.

How did the wayfaring Odin discover the runes? In his own words he tells of the mystery that was revealed in a sacrificial experience which in some aspects is almost akin to the suffering of Jesus on the cross.

> —I trow that I hung on the windy tree,
> Swing there nights all nine,
> gashed with a blade,
> bloodied for Odin,
> myself an offering to myself —
> knotted to that tree,
> no man knows
> whither the roots of it run.

None gave me bread
none gave me drink,
down to the depths
I peered
to snatch up Runes,
with a roaring scream
and fell in a dizzied swoon.

Well-being I won
and wisdom too,
I grew and joyed in my growth –
from a word to a word
I was led to a word,
from a deed to another deed.

Versions of this self-sacrifice by Odin survived in badly
garbled form to Christian times. One of these was inspired by
an Anglo-Saxon charm calling for the gathering of nine
different herbs. Two of these are described as follows.

'Thyme and Fennel, a pair great in power,
the wise Lord, holy in heaven,
wrought these herbs while hung on the cross –
he placed them and put them in the
seven worlds,
to aid all, rich and poor.'

At first reading one would be forgiven for dismissing this as
a hybrid Christian charm and the terms 'wise Lord' and 'hung
on the cross' could be read quite innocently as references to
the crucifixion of Jesus. However, the words 'seven worlds'
betray this rhyme's pagan meaning, for these were the seven
planes of existence described in Scandinavian myths. The
'wise Lord, holy in heaven' is none other than Odin, who hung
on the tree to gain the rune wisdom. Christianization of pagan
rites and rhymes was sometimes encouraged by secret
followers of the old religion, for it hid their activities from
prying eyes. Unfortunately this process became destructive.
The true pagan magic was lost by people who no longer
understood the secret teachings obscured by the veneer of
orthodox Christian belief.

Another example of Christian-pagan blends is the following

Photograph by courtesy of the Manx Museum

Thorwald's cross-slab, dating from the tenth century, shows a graphic scene from Ragnarök, the last great battle of Norse pagan mythology. Odin, recognized by the raven on his shoulder, is devoured by the Fenris wolf.

charm to ward off evil. A horseshoe – symbolic of the crescent moon and the horned god – was fixed to the door lintel with three virgin nails from the local blacksmith. As the nails were hammered in the following verse was recited.

Father, Son and Holy Ghost,
Nail the Devil to the post,
Thrice I smite with Holy Crook,
With this mell I thrice do knock,
Once for God and one for Wod,
And once for Lok.

As it is hardly likely that the person would have used a crucifix to hammer in the nails, the reference to a 'holy crook' seems suspect. I postulate that it is an oblique reference either to the sacred hammer of the Norse god Thor or the runic swastika – sometimes known as the *crooked cross*.

The last two lines invoking both Woden and his brother Loki suggest that the charm is a bastardized pagan spell, and it is interesting to note in folklore records that this charm is still in current use – to ward off witches on Hallowe'en night and prevent the evil eye from harming cattle and other livestock. Old spells die hard.

In a more traditional and conventional form the legend of Odin's rune-making adventures can be found on a Manx standing-stone, which gives his name and a description of his herioc deeds in a runic script, together with carved illustrations of the one-eyed god and his pet raven. We can compare Odin's death on the tree with the myth of the sacrificed Celtic god mentioned earlier. He is bloodied, cut with a knife, probably intoxicated with mead or some other sacred potion and left to hang bleeding while his life force fertilizes the soil. During his death and rebirth on the cross, Odin experiences the sacred mysteries of the runes and passes the truths received to his mortal believers.

The Old Religion

If we examine myths such as these, from different stages in the rise of the European tribes, we can see the way that individual racial beliefs synthesize with others and that they all owe their origin to some central ritual source. This embryonic cauldron of religious inspiration originated with Stone Age man and is defined today under the generic heading of the *old religion*, compassing the earliest beliefs of ancient man and his recurring myth of the sky father and earth mother – the divine couple who are aspects of the one life force which created and sustained the universe. The advent of Christianity largely destroyed this important outlook on the natural world, although degraded forms of the old beliefs did materialise in medieval Europe. By then they were already modified and adapted by foreign influences, and were quickly exorcised from the racial consiousness by the servants of the new faith. Rumours persist that the true beliefs still survive in isolated places today but the seeker is likely to discover only the revived debased versions of the old ways in his search for the ancient truths.

Although runes had their historical origins in the Bronze and Iron Ages, they first were noticed in the form we recognize in the early centuries AD around Northern Italy and Southern Germany. It is often claimed that runic writing was a clumsy attempt by primitive people to copy the Latin alphabet, but a very early form of runic alphabet was discovered at Alvae in Portugal dating from Neolithic times. It is therefore more logical to assume that our modern alphabet is derived from the rune system and not the other way around.

Fupark

The early Germanic rune alphabet, regarded as the earliest example of true runes, was termed *fupark* (the p pronounced as th) and this name was taken from its first six letters. The fupark alphabet moved both west and north and was soon well established in the magical curriculum of both the Scandinavian and Saxon races. Adaptations were made in local usage but the basic design and layout of the rune symbols remained the same all over the Continent.

One of the first points of interest in runic writing is the strong, masculine, very angular strokes employed and the squaring off on the letters, which is a characteristic unique to runes. It is speculated, (as is so much about this subject) that the unusual shape of the letters arose from the original practice of carving the symbols onto hard wood and was dictated by the heavy incising with a knife blade needed to make a mark. This practice would have ruled out rounded or curved signs for practical reasons. Each rune word was read either from left to right or right to left and each was separated from the other by a plain dot. When Christianity swallowed up the runes, equal-armed cross symbols replaced the dots, but even these vanished when the Church decided that runes were a danger to the mortal soul and banned their study and use.

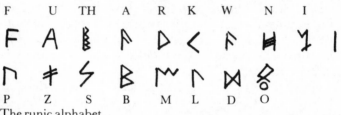

The runic alphabet.

Sometimes runes were engraved on metal or leather and then coloured in a red pigment. In Scandinavia witches using the runes to curse an enemy mixed human blood to colour the symbols. Such unpleasant practices indicate the occult powers believed to exist in the runes; and illustrate the old belief that any magical object or symbol anointed with human blood would have more potency in occult rituals.

It is difficult to give the precise date when the runic alphabet was introduced into Anglo-Saxon England but we can be sure that the fupark system was brought here by the Saxon pirates who modified it to suit their own needs and tastes. When the Vikings began their forages to the English coast, and eventually established settlements here on occupied land they introduced the Scandinavian runes, which would then have fused with the runic alphabets already here.

Whatever type of rune we find, each had its secret meaning based on the magico-religious philosophy of the people who utilized it. Listed below are the Germanic runes with their corresponding Anglo-Saxon names and magical symbolism.

ᛒ   *Beorc* referred to the birch tree and the fertility rites of spring.

ᚢ *Ur* meant 'wild oxen' and these were the animals used as sacrifices to the gods.

ᚡ *Feoh* signified the cattle, an important feature in the economy of any ancient peoples.

ᚦ *Porn* was a giant or demon believed to haunt the dark Nordic forests. The Old English story of *Beowulf* is an example of the struggle between good and evil, represented by the warrior hero and the supernatural monster. Use of this rune could, so it was believed, evoke such a demon from the underworld.

ᚩ *Os* meant simply a god and can be used to invoke or refer to any member of the Norse mythology.

ᚱ *Rad* was a long journey on horseback and in the magical, mythical language of the runes it could be the soul's last journey to the underworld after death.

ᚲ *Ken*, a torch and light, was a masculine symbol of the sun in pagan days. In Europe the practice of kindling bonfires at solstice and equinox was carried forward from Celtic observance into the Middle Ages and as a folklore art form has been revived recently. This relic of ancient fire worship is denoted by this rune sign.

ᚷ *Gyfu*, a gift to the gods, was a euphemism for the sacrifice of an animal or human volunteer at one of the major rites.

ᚹ *Wyn* meant joy or glory. Odin performed his rune magic with some twigs refered to as 'Glory Wands', so there may be an occult meaning to that word which is as yet undiscovered.

ᚺ *Haegl* was ice or hail, the natural weapons of the frost giants and other icy denizens of the otherworlds.

ᚾ *Nyd* was the need or necessity which drives a man to accomplish impossible deeds in order to survive. In Saxon villages the need to survive was acute, as the dangers faced included famine, disease and attacks from marauding pirates.

ᛄ *Ger*, a spear, principal weapon of both Odin and the war god Tew (who gave his name to Tuesday), was an object carried into battle by nearly every Saxon and Norse warrior.

ᛇ *Eoh* Yew meant a wood sacred to runecraft and carved into rune wands. It had connections with the dead and even today we find yew trees growing in country churchyards as if guarding the deceased.

ᛈ *Pear* is a mystery name in the rune alphabet. So far it has baffled translators.

ᛉ *Eolh* meant defence or protection. A rune for magic to keep away unwanted influences, or trespassers from property. Linked with the magical sign of the splayed hand as a gesture to ward off the evil eye.

ᛉ *Sigel* meant, literally, the sun, the principal object of pagan worship.

↑ *Tir* was the war god Tew. Runes of this shape were carved on the amulets of Norsemen to protect them from harm in battle and to give them strength and courage.

ᛗ *Man* was quite straightforward and could refer either to the individual or the race as a collective entity.

ᚲ *Lagu*, or water, the sacred liquid, signified the womb of the great mother from whence all life came.

ᛢ *Ing* meant the Danes.

ᛟ *Epel* represented inherited land or property.

ᛞ *Doeg* was the day, when the sun was at its most powerful and all good magic could be performed.

If the meaning of these rune words is examined it can be clearly seen how they were used for magical and divinatory purposes. Individual letters and combinations of letters were grouped together to form mystical incantations for cursing, healing, defending, attacking and predicting by those adept in the arts of rune casting and making.

I will examine the rune masters and spells wrought by the application of runic knowledge in the next chapter.

3.

THE RUNE MASTERS

Odin, the dark god of Norse mythology was the divine instrument through whom the runes were given to mankind and he was the first rune master of many to follow. The mystical cult of Odin, which was widespread in Norway, Denmark and Sweden and taken to other lands by the Vikings or Norse sea pirates, numbered in its ranks magicians, seers and wizards skilled in the secret art of runecraft.

Old Odin himself was said to possess the power to raise the dead, divine the future, fly through the sky and change his shape at will, so that he travelled undetected in the form of a wolf, raven or eagle. He possessed these supernatural powers because of his knowledge of runes and promised the same gifts to his earthly followers who administered the dark mysteries of the one-eyed god's rites. In his own words Odin told his worshippers the powers and knowledge they were expected to gain before they could call themselves priests of his cult.

Ye shall find runes and signs to read,
Signs most mighty, signs so strong,
which the soothsayer coloured, the High
Gods made,
and the Old Ones carved.
Do ye know how they should be carved?
Do ye know how they should be read?
Do ye know how they should be coloured?
Do ye know how they should be tried?

Questions such as these would have been posed to the candidate entering the Odic mysteries and he would have been asked to give the correct responses before admission to the cult was granted. We can only guess at the nature of the initiation ceremony for new priests but can surmise that it would have included a symbolic sacrifice by hanging from a yew tree, in imitation of the greater sacrifice of the one-eyed god.

In the public ceremonies of Odin worship human sacrifices were sometimes offered. Criminals guilty of capital offences, or captured prisoners-of-war, were sentenced to be ritually sacrified and the killing was accomplished by the priests of Odin, who strangled the victims with leather thongs. Nordic monuments often depict scenes of ritual hanging, dating from the Viking Age, and the discovery of mummified victims of strangulation in Danish peat bogs suggests that these sacrifices date back to the Bronze Age.

When the victim was neither a criminal nor a POW it was not unknown for the ruling king to elect to die for his people. He became a human representative of the god dying, so that the tribe could have a fertile harvest and good fishing. Ceremonies of this type were not uncommon in pagan times when the monarch was regarded as the divine incarnation of the tribal god. The memory of such beliefs lingered on in the Middle Ages in the divine right of kings and the superstition that diseases could be cured by the touch of royalty.

In some cases the royal victim was unready to sacrifice himself for the good of his people and saw no reason why he should die because he was unfortunate enough to be of royal birth. Such a person was King Vikar of Norway, who was offered as a sacrifice to Odin and tried to fake the event to escape death. Vikar stood on a rotten tree stump under a weak tree branch, secured by a soft noose of calf gut and with a henchman ready to strike him with a slender reed. Unfortunately, the reed suddenly changed into a sharp stake, the tree stump crumbled under his feet, the noose tightened into a strong cord and the branch sprung up, impaling the hapless coward on the stake. Odin was not so easily cheated of his offering of human blood.

Supernatural Swords and Shields

The cult of Odin, deity of death in battle, had its own warrior caste know as *berserkers* from the Nordic for 'bear shirt' or 'wolf skin', referring to the shaggy animal pelts they wore in battle. These men were fanatical disciples of Odin and their sword hilts and blades were engraved with runic inscriptions exorting them to do battle in honour of the travelling god. From the descriptions of such swords came the legends of magical weapons which thirsted for blood and which, once unleashed, killed at random anyone who came in their way. Excalibur, the sword of the British warlord Arthur Pendragon, was one of these invincible weapons and was apparently of supernatural origin.

On their round shields, made from strips of seasoned wood, the warriors of Odin painted the runic sigil ↑ signifying the god of war. Any man who carried such a sign in battle was reputed to possess incredible strength and courage, for no enemy could overcome the deadly magic of the Norse battle runes. The berserkers glady charged the oncoming foe without thought for their own safety, confident that Odin and the powers of the runes would protect them from harm.

Under their bestial disguises the berserkers were naked. Popular legend said they could change shape at will into bears and wolves by using secret runes granted by Odin. Such beliefs arose from the speed that the warriors could don and doff their animal pelts and their bloodchilling battle cries, imitating the howling of wolves and the snarling of bears.

Apart from the berserkers, the other rune masters were the ordinary local priests of Odin who tended the temples and groves sacred to the god's worship and ministered to the congregations. In Sweden the disciples of the old gods were called *Attiba* or wizards and are described as follows by an overseas visitor to the Scandinavian settlements.

> They have their Attiba who have authority over them as masters for they order them to make offerings of men, cattle and grain as they please. When they have chosen who or what they want then the offering is taken away for sacrifice.

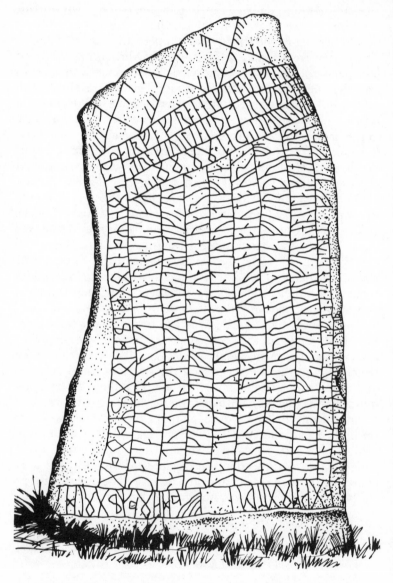

Swedish standing stone inscribed with runic symbols.

Thuls and Finns

In Denmark the priests of the old religion were called *thuls* meaning 'reciter of incantations' and they were regarded as magicians with a great knowledge of runecraft. In addition to these orthodox priests there were lay practitioners of rune magic and in many cases these people were referred to simply as *Finns*, a general term for the Laplanders who originally settled in Scandinavia in prehistoric times. The Finns were held in awe by the Nordic tribes as natural magicians and their skill with runes and enchantments was feared and respected.

These witches and sorcerers were direct descendants of the shamans, or priest-magicians, of the Bronze Age whose remains have been preserved in Danish burial mounds. One of these burial sites was discovered in the closing years of the nineteenth century at Lyngby, near Copenhagen. Inside the oak coffin the archaeologists found a 'magic bag' owned by the Bronze Age wizard. The bag contained a number of strange objects including some amber beads (as revered by the Celts some centuries later) a conch shell, a falcon's claw, the bones of a snake, a bronze dagger, a squirrel's skull and the dried intestines of a small rodent. The scientists who opened this mound were convinced that this was the last resting place of a local magician and the conclusion was confirmed when they discovered near the body a forked hazel twig, wrapped in animal skin, which they identified as a magic wand.

The shamans and rune masters of the ancient Nordic lands were easily recognizable by the unique clothing which marked their profession. They wore bizarre head-dresses made from the pelts of woodland creatures, a woollen cloak – dyed blue, the sacred colour of Odin – and carried a leather pouch filled with herbs and charms hung from a staff carved with runic sigils.

In a manuscript entitled *The Saga Of Erik The Red* written in the thirteenth century the anonymous writer gives a graphic description of a seeress or mistress of runecraft.

She wore a cloak set with stones along the hem, around her neck and covering her head (was) a hood lined with white catskin. In one hand she carried a staff with a knob at the end and at her belt, holding together her long dress, was a charm pouch. She wore calfskin shoes and catskin mittens to cover her hands at all times.

Another of these rune seers is described in the words of the following Icelandic song recited by a sybil, a woman who could see into the future and divine the destiny of men.

Hedi, men call me when their homes I visit,
A far seeing witch, wise in talismans,
caster of spells, cunning in magic,
to wicked women welcome always.

Arm rings and necklaces, Odin ye gave me,
to learn my love, to learn all magics,
wider and wider, through all worlds I see.

Outside I sat myself when ye came,
terror of the Gods and gazed into mine eyes,
What do ye ask of me?
Why tempt me?

Odin – I know where thy lost eye
has gone,
hidden away in Mimir's well,
Mimir each morn his mead he drinks,
Well, would ye know more?

The reference in the third verse which says 'Outside I sat myself when ye came' refers to a period of isolation practised by ancient magicians during which their spirits were liberated from the body and communed with the gods. It is a common magical practice of the North American Indians and is not unknown in the present-day witch covens of the European cult of witchcraft.

In the last verse, the seeress boasts to Odin that she is as wise as he, for she knows where his lost eye has gone. In the Norse myths Odin sacrificed an eye to the god Mimir, who guarded the well of wisdom and knowledge (similar to the 'cauldron of inspiration' stirred by the Celtic moon goddess Ceridwen) in exchange for forbidden magical lore.

The Potency of Runecraft

Runecraft was so potent that the use of an incorrect rune by someone could cause the most terrible disaster and it was essential that the practitioner was skilled in his or her art. It was definitely a case of a little learning being a dangerous thing, for the use of a cursing rune where a healing one was needed had obvious fatal consequences. In such a happening the relatives of the deceased might decide to wet their swords with the blood of the guilty rune master.

In one of the old Nordic sagas, a rune master called Egill is called to the house of a sick woman. He soon deduces that the patient's recovery is impeded by the actions of a rival wizard. The opposing magician had carved the incorrect runes on a piece of whale bone hanging over the woman's bed and this makes Egill pronounce scorn on those who were fain to use runecraft but lacked the skill for their safe and correct magical application.

> Runes shall a man not score,
> save he can read them well,
> that many a man betideth,
> on a mirk stave to stumble,
> saw I on a scraped whale bone,
> ten dark staves scored,
> thou hath to the leek widen
> over long sickness broughten.

The magician immediately scores out the negative runic charm and engraves the proper words on the bone, which he then places under the sick woman's pillow. Within minutes she awakes as if from a long sleep and is completely healed of her ailment.

At another time, Egill used his knowledge of runes to discover that his drink had been poisoned by a magical rival. He scored runic signs on the rim of the suspect drinking horn and reddened these with his own blood. At once the vessel broke in two and the drink was scattered to the four winds. If the liquid had been pure and undefiled the runes would have had no effect on the horn.

It is evident that when the Viking pirates went on raiding

trips abroad they took with them a rune master to divine the omens and protect them from Celtic and Saxon magic. Evidence of such a practice can be found in the runic graffiti carved by Norse raiders inside a Neolithic tomb in the Orkney Isles. One of these inscriptions records the fact that, 'That man most skilled in runecraft west over the sea cut these', which shows no little modesty on the part of the carver!

It is possible that the person who carved these runes may not have been a priest-magician of Odin, for the making of runes was not confined to initiated members of the priesthood. Earl Rognvald of the Orkneys is quoted as boasting.

> There are nine skills known to me –
> at tables I play ably,
> rarely I run out of runes,
> reading, smith, craft, both come ready,
> I can skim the ground on skis,
> weld a bow, do well in rowing,
> to both arts I bend my mind,
> poet's lay and harper's playing.

However, it is certain that the initiated rune master held an important rank in pagan society. Without his knowledge, inspiration and insight, the ordinary folk faced with the evoked powers of the runes would have been helpless. Only one skilled in the art of runecraft could safely translate and interpret the magical meanings of runes and steer a safe course through their magical maze for others to follow. It is hardly surprising that the great rune masters – such as Egill – were promoted to the status of semi-divine hero figures and had epic poems and sagas woven around their exploits.

4.

CASTING THE RUNES

A person living in the twentieth century has little conception of the influence and power exerted by magic in the lives of his ancestors, even up to fairly recent times. Religious practices of the past, which usually included magical rituals, were not regarded, as they are today, as a once-a-week observance of the hypothetical existence of a supreme creator but as a daily acknowledgement of the powers of nature which ruled the lives of men. Magic was as normal and as acceptable to our ancient predecessors as electricity is to us today, and in their eyes just as vital to the sustaining of everyday life. It was pure commonsense to the ancient peoples of Western Europe to invoke their gods and placate them with magical rites in order to ward off illness, bring good luck and fertility to the tribe and maintain harmony between men and the natural forces which they regarded as supernatural manifestations of the gods.

In Western Europe, during the historical period we now designate as the Dark Ages, the most powerful form of magic was that of the secret craft of rune casting. The use of runes achieved such a wide popularity because, unlike the later magical traditions of the Middle Ages which drew their impetus from the Judeo-Christian cabbala, it was a magic system with down-to-earth symbols relating to daily life.

The scope of runic magic is emphasized by the following list of different runes taken from the Norse sagas: birth runes, healthy runes, battle runes, fertility runes, weather runes, love runes, healing runes, cursing runes and death runes. All these symbols and their attendant powers for good or evil were available to the ordinary person, either directly or through the offices of a local wizard, rune master or priest.

Rune sorcery was considered so potent that even the dead could be raised by their evocation. This necromantic rite of the dead was celebrated in a popular rhyme attributed to Odin.

> A twelfth spell know I,
> when I see aloft a tree,
> a corpse swinging from a rope,
> then I cut and paint runes,
> so the man walks,
> and speaks with me.

As well as reviving the departed, runes were carved within graves to ward off tomb robbers and demons, just as in Ancient Egypt burial places were decorated with magical heiroglyphics to seal the mummies from harm. The Norse and Teutonic grave inscriptions were engraved 'not in day nor with an iron knife'. Night was the obvious time when conjurations could be worked to aid the dead and iron was the only metal which could injure the faery people of the departed, so its use was forbidden in or near burial mounds. This strange belief dates from the discovery of iron in addition to bronze when legends grew up about the users of the 'old' metal, who became regarded by the Iron Age people as supernatural folk or kin to the faeries.

Runes were also carved on gravestones marking the burial sites of famous kings, warriors or magicians. The symbols could either be simple epitaphs reciting the deceased person's deeds, or incantations to protect the spirit on its journey to the underworld.

Runic Self-Defence
In addition to protecting those who had left the earthly realm, runes had the power to ward off evil and bad luck from the living. Both Norsemen and Saxons believed in the *wyrd* which

Panel of the Anglo-Saxon Franks casket, showing scenes of 'The Adoration of the Magi' and 'Wayland the smith' surrounded by a runic inscription.

translated into modern English is fate or destiny. In pagan times the word was associated with a triple goddess (featured by William Shakespeare in his play *Macbeth* as the witches on the moor of the 'three weird sisters') whose three aspects were known as the weavers or 'spinners of the fate of men'. When the old religion went underground in the early Middle Ages the concept of the wyrd remained as the avenging finger of death, sent by Jehovah to punish the Christian wicked.

While the Norse and Saxon peoples believed implicitly in the power of destiny and accepted that the soul's fate was mapped out before birth, they also believed that evil could be averted and supernatural forces deflected by the use of powerful magic such as the runes. Many of the burial mounds and graves of the period preceding Christianity contain brooches, pendants and rings engraved with runic symbols and these were clearly worn to protect the wearer from harm. A selection of rune rings unearthed at a Saxon burial can be seen in the British Museum and are fine examples of this type of magical self-defence.

The markings on the amulets consist of either a single rune such as *Eolh* Ψ which stands for 'defence' or 'protection' or a set of runes forming a word believed to have efficacy over the forces of evil. As each rune has a different meaning, the possible permutations available covered every sphere of human activity and could be re-arranged and added to in order to produce a variety of results.

Wyrd was also associated with the runes as a system of divining or predicting the future. Today many thousands of people visit astrologers and palmists to see how lady luck (the wyrd?) is going to treat them: in the Dark Ages the seeker of future portents consulted the rune caster to look into the coming time. Rune divination was practised in two ways, by twigs and by stones, both objects revered by pagans as the residing places of sacred powers.

One of the simplest ways to cast the runes was to cut the bark from a tree and slice it into strips. These were marked with runes and then scattered over a white cloth laid on the ground. The diviner called on the gods, made a sacrifice of a small animal and then picked up three bark strips at random.

The selected strips were then interpreted in relation to the question posed by the client.

In the second method, runes were painted on one side of smooth, flat pebbles which were shaken up in a leather bag and then cast on the ground. Whatever runes were showing when the stones landed referred to the matter under divination.

Yew or hazel wood staves were employed by the rune masters because they linked with Odin, as did most aspects of rune lore. The story is told that the one-eyed god 'took nine glory twigs and smote an adder and it flew into nine parts'. Translated, the riddle means that the hooded god carried nine rune wands with which he hit the snake and cut it into pieces. Obviously the adder would have died from such blows anyway but, if you accepted the omnipotent power of runes, then you believed that the poor creature was killed by magic and not the terrible physical injuries inflicted upon it.

Runes were used to attract a lover and one famous spell is recited in an Old English poem *The Husband's Wife* which states 'follow the sun's path south across the ocean to find joy with the man who is waiting there'. Such happy runes as these are rare, for both the Norse and Saxon were fighting people and the majority of their runes are dominated by references to war, battles and victory.

Jutish sword carved with its name, 'Increase To Pain', and 'Woe to the weapons of the foe' in runic symbols.

Sword Runes

In the previous chapter we mentioned the carving of runes on
the hilts and blades of swords. An example of this craft was
found on an iron weapon dug up on the Isle of Wight. The
sword is Jutish and incised on it are the words 'Woe to the
weapons of the foe', together with its name 'Increase To Pain',
which is a chilling description of the object as a weapon of
injury and death. Another example of sword runes is found on
a broken blade dredged up from the bed of the River Thames.
It is over two feet in length, engraved with the twenty-eight
symbols of a complete runic alphabet and the name of its
owner. This unusual sword is regarded by some experts as the
Rosetta-stone of the runic script and it is a wonderful epitaph
to the skill of both sword maker and rune caster.

To illustrate the wider adoption of runes in Scandanavian
magic consider the following poem taken from a Norse saga,
evidently addressed by a rune master to his pupil.

> Runes of war, know thee well,
> if great thou wilt be,
> cut them on hilt of hardened sword,
> some on the brand's back,
> some on shining side,
> twice the name Tew thereon.
>
> Sea runes good at need
> learn for ship's saving,
> for good health of swimming horse –
> on the stern cut them,
> cut them on rudder blade.
>
> Word runes, learn ye well,
> if thou cant that no man,
> shalt pay back grief thou gavest,
> wind thou these, weave thou these,
> Cast thou these about ye,
> at the Thing where folk do throng,
> into the full doom faring.
>
> Of ale runes know the wisdom,
> if thou wilt another's wife,

should not bewy thy heart,
cut them on yon mead horn,
on the back of each hand,
and nicked upon thy nail.

Help runes shalt thou gather,
if skill thou would'st gain
to loosen child from low-lain mother,
Cut they be in hands hollow,
wrapped the joints round about,
call for the good folk's aid and help.

Learn the bough runes' wisdom,
if leech lore thou lovest,
and wilt wot wounds searching
on the bark they be scored,
on the buds of trees,
whose boughs look eastward ever.

Thought runes shalt thou deal with,
if thou wilt be of all men purest-
souled right and wise,
those creded, those first out,
those first took to heart.

On the shield were they scored,
that stands before the Shining God,
on Early-Waking's oar,
on All Knowing's hoof,
on the wheel which runneth
under Regnir's chariot,
on Sleipnir's jaw teeth,
on the sleigh traces,
on the rough bear's paws,
and on Bragi's tongue,
on the wolf claw,
on the eagle's bill,
on bloody wing,
and bridge's end,
on loosing palms,
and pity's path.

On glass, on gold
and goodly silver.
in wine and in wort
and the seat of the witch wife,
on Gungnir's point
and Grani's bosom,
on the Norm's nail
and the neb of the night owl.

All these so cut,
were shaven and heared
and mingled with holy mead,
and sent upon wide ways,
some bide with elves –
some with the Aesir
or wise Vanir,
or some still hold the sons of men.

These be the book runes
and runes of good help,
and all the ale runes
and runes of much might,
to whom they may so avail,
unbewitched, unspoilt,
they are wholesome to have,
thrive thou with these then –
when thou hast learnt their lore,
till the Gods end thy life days.

This description of the runes and their uses illustrates the varied purposes they were put to in ancient times and if ever there was a natural magic of the common people then the casting of runes would be it. There are few clues in the writings on runes that there were ever any higher mysteries associated with the subject and in nearly every case runes are evoked for material purposes. The motives behind rune casting appear purely selfish and there is no whisper of any aim or rune magic other than bettering the conditions of the user on earth. Certainly there is no room in runic lore for the airy-fairy speculations and pseudo-mystical imaginings of certain types of medieval magic, which concentrate on the spiritual condition of the soul and lose sight of the material goals in the present life span.

In the third verse above there is an interesting mention of runes made 'on the back of the hand and nicked upon the nail'. This would indicate that some kind of runic tatoo could have been worn by magicians and others. Ritual scarification was common in many pagan cultures and is still seen today in scarring ceremonies enacted by African tribes when a boy reaches the age of maturity. Magical tatoos were a feature of Celtic life and were achieved by cutting the skin and mixing woad into the wounds to cause coloured scars. It is interesting to speculate whether the so-called *diablo stigmata* or 'devil's mark', reputed in the Middle Ages to have been given to the witches by their horned god, was in fact a cult tatoo. If so, it might well have been of a runic nature, for we know that runecraft survived into the medieval period.

The archetypal rune master, Odin, also revealed his knowledge of how to carve runes and the various forms of magic which could be worked with them by a skilled adept.

> Know how to cut them,
> know how to read them,
> know how to stain them,
> know how to evoke them,
> know how to send them.
>
> Better not to ask than to overpledge,
> as a gift demands a gift,
> better not to slay than to slay too many.
>
> The first charm I know
> is unknown to all,
> of any of human kind,
> 'Help' it is named,
> for help it gives,
> in hours of anguish,
> and in sorrow.
>
> I know a second –
> that those that would be leeches
> must learn,

I know a third – in battle,
if need be great, it blunts,
the swords of enemies,
so there are no wounds.

I know a fourth,
which frees me quickly,
if foes should bind me first,
a chant I know
that breaks fetters,
burst bonds.

A fifth – no arrow
hurts if shot,
no spear kills,
if thrown,
no stone hurts,
if pitched.

I know a sixth –
if runes are cut to harm me,
the spell is turned,
the hunger harmed,
not I.

I know a seventh rune –
if a hall blazes around
my bench mates,
though hot the flames,
they feel nought.

I know an eighth –
if hate festers in a warrior's heart,
my spell will calm him.

I know a ninth –
when need of it.
to shelter my ship from winter storm,
the wind it calms,
the waves abate,
the sea is put to sleep.

I know a tenth rune –
if spirits trouble,

I work, they wander afar,
unable to find form or home.

I know an eleventh –
when I lead in battle
and unwounded I go to war,
unscathed I return.

I know a twelfth –
when I see aloft a tree,
a corpse swinging from a rope,
then I cut and paint runes,
so the man walks,
and speaks with me.

I know a thirteenth –
if I cast runes
a warrior will not fall in battle,
or die by sword cut.

I know a fourteenth –
that few know,
if I tell a troop of warriors
about the Old Ones, gods or elves,
I can name them all.

I know a fifteenth –
sung to the gods,
gives power to men,
prowess to elves,
foresight to all by Odin's gift.

I know a seventeenth –
that binds the hearts,
charms the young girls,
releases love.

I know an eighteenth –
that is never told,
a secret hidden from all.
except the love in my arms,
or my sister.

An interesting point to notice in this mammoth list of accomplishments is the second verse which clearly warns of the dangers inherent in rune magic. 'Better not to ask than overpledge, as a gift demands a gift.' At first glance these seem innocent words till you realise that it is a warning that whoever uses the runes to become too wealthy will lose something in return, something he or she dearly loves, for 'a gift demands a gift'. It was an ancient belief that if a person was too lucky or successful then something they loved, such as a spouse or child, would be taken from them by the gods as the price of success.

A sublimated belief in this type of occurrence still exists today and is exemplified by stories of pacts with the devil, which give material pleasures in life but demand the soul of the hedonist on death. It is also found in the old saying used when a person inherits money, that 'no good will come of it', and the fateful events which often follow such inheritances prove the truth of this saying.

In the second part of this verse the erratic nature of runes and their occult powers is demonstrated in the words, 'better not to slay than to slay too many'. Once unleashed, the killing runes were obviously very unpredictable and were indiscriminate in their choice of victim.

'Casting the Runes'

The classic ghost story 'Casting the Runes' by M.R. James – filmed in the 1950s as *The Night of the Demon* – featured the strange powers of the death runes. In the story the sorcerer passes the runes to his victims on a scrap of paper and they experience a horrible death. He is finally outwitted by the hero who, having received the runic curse, manages to slip the paper back to the magician, who falls victim to the nameless 'thing' evoked by the ancient spell. All very neat, but unfortunately evidence suggests that the death runes were not so easily controlled as in M.R. James's famous story.

Great care was needed to restrain their powers, as is true of any magical force evoked by the magician or witch today.

5.

RUNIC SURVIVALS

It is not surprising that when Christianity came to the lands ruled by Saxon and Norseman the magical craft of runes was slow to die out, even though the Church eventually condemned it as the practice of black magic.

As late as the seventeenth century, rune magic was openly practised in pagan Iceland, a country where even today paganism is still alive. So tenacious to the casting of runes were the Icelanders, that the clerical authorities were forced to impose the death penalty on anyone found dabbling in the forbidden art. This edict had little effect, for rune magic still survives in Iceland where recently the people celebrated a revival of interest in the old religion.

When the early Christian missionaries arrived in this country they found that the pagan beliefs still permeated everyday life. The clerical historian, Bede, noted in AD 679 that when a.young Northumbrian captive slipped his fetters he was asked, 'hwaeoer he pa alysendlecan rune cuoe and pa stafas mid him awritene haefde', or, translated from Old English, 'whether he knew the loosening runes and had about him the (magical) letters written down'.

Christian prayers often took over pagan incantations but there is an interesting case where this process was reversed and the Lord's Prayer written in runes was used by pagans as a battle spell to ensure victory. So prevalent were such abuses that as late as the eleventh century an Abbot Aelfric spoke a sermon denouncing 'outh drycraft oe outh runstafum' or 'the magic through runes'. His edict would have been directed against such Saxon charms as the following one for healing burns.

> Three Ladies came out of the east,
> with snow, frost and fire,
> out fire – in frost,
> by the names of Woden, Thor and Lok.

In later versions of the spell the last offending line was erased in favour of an invocation to 'Father, Son and Holy Ghost'.

This Roman tessellated pavement, discovered at Aldborough, incorporates the swastika design.

Old and New Beliefs

During the eight and ninth centuries in Christianized parts of the country cemeteries exhibited gravestones carved with prayers to the departed in runic script. This was just one way that Christian priests adapted the old beliefs of the people and transformed them into acceptable forms suited to the ideology of the new faith. Evidence of this compromise is given in an extract from a letter by Pope Gregory to Abbot Melluis on his departure to Britain in AD 601.

I have come to the conclusion that the idols among the people should on no account be destroyed, but the temples themselves should be aspersed with holy water, altars set up in them and relics deposited there. For if these temples are well built they must be purified from the worship of demons and dedicated to the service of God. In this way, we hope that the people, seeing their temples are not destroyed, may abandon their error and flocking more readily to their accustomed resorts many come to know and adore the true God.

And since they have the custom of sacrificing many oxen to demons, let some other solemnity be substituted in its place, such as a day of dedication or festivals of the holy matyrs whose relics are preserved there. On such occasions they may well construct shelters of boughs for themselves around the churches that once were temples and celebrate with devout feasting. They are no longer to sacrifice beasts to the Devil but may kill them for food to the praise of God.

Such edicts must have created some strange precedents, as pagan ritual mingled with Christian prayers to the glory of God, Jesus and the saints. Pagan temples could be found which had two altars, one for the celebration of the mass and the other for sacrificing animals to the pagan gods. The Saxon church at Bishopstone in Sussex shows a later adaptation of this type of combined worship, for in the porch is a small niche that at one time held the effigy of a pagan god. As the congregation entered the church they first made their offering according to the rites of the Old Religion, before kneeling at the altar of the new faith. At Knowlton in Dorset there are the ruins of a Norman church built within a pre-Christian

Crown copyright: reproduced by permission of the Department of the Environment.

Detail of the Ruthwell Cross.

earthwork circle and there is evidence that the site was still
used for pagan worship in the eleventh century.

The Ruthwell Cross

Some of the Saxon pagans were quite happy to accept Jesus as
another form of the sacrificed god Odin. A cross dating from
AD 750 was discovered in a church at Ruthwell, Dumfries,
and is inscribed with runes describing the death of Jesus, as
told in the Christian poem called *The Dream Of The Rood*. The
Ruthwell Cross is also decorated with pagan motifs showing
birds, animals and foliage, together with scenes from the
gospels included the nativity, the flight to Egypt, the baptism
by St John, the healing of a blind man by Jesus, Mary
Magdelene washing the feet of her Master and the crucifixion.

In the seventeenth century, the cross was torn down and
smashed by Puritans who regarded it as 'an idolatrous
monument'. It is doubtful if they could read the runes on its
side and probably mistook the object for an heathen standing-
stone. Alternatively they may have understood its secret
message and seen the pagan references to the hanging of Odin
on the wisdom tree mingled with the Christian content.

Fortunately, the cross was rediscovered in 1802, the broken
fragments were collected together and placed in their present
resting place within the church, to be preserved for those
moderns who appreciate its value as a symbol of the fusing of
pagan and Christian elements in Anglo-Saxon culture.

Runes in general survived the coming of Jesus until the
seventeenth century, as we have seen in Iceland. In Norway,
another northern country where old beliefs died hard, the
runes were used for both esoteric and exoteric purposes up to
the twelfth and thirteenth centuries. The Church's
determined efforts to suppress the runes and replace them
with the Latin alphabet can be regarded as proof not only of
the clerical fear of pagan magic but the Catholic priest's belief
in the occult powers associated with the rune symbols.

Condemnation of the runes as magical signs eventually
became mixed up with the medieval heresy of witchcraft and
by the time of the great witch hunts of the fifteenth and
sixteenth centuries the lore of runes was largely forgotten in

most parts of Europe. They lived on only in the archives of monasteries, where eccentric monks busied themselves with research into obscure subjects, including runes, although they knew that they risked excommunication or death if their hobby was discovered. By the late Middle Ages runes were regarded as a sign of dabbling in the black arts and their discovery on a person was regarded as proof of involvement in witchcraft and devil worship.

Runes, however, survived in a curious way, as they were adopted by the lodges of *speculative* freemasonry which arose from the craftsmen's guilds in medieval towns. Unfortunately, their use does not seem to have survived as far as modern masonry, not even in the occult orientated lodges of the co-masons founded by Annie Besant and connected with the Theosophical Society and the Masonic Grand Orient of France.

Masons' Pentagrams

Certain runes were adopted as *mason's marks* by medieval stone-workers and these were introduced into the great European cathedrals and churches. Pentagrams and other magical insignia were also carved on stones by the masons as trade marks, pointing to a belief in magical lore far superseding the present-day mumbo-jumbo of the freemason lodge.

In the sixteenth century, the Danish admiral of the fleet, Mogens Gyldenstjene, used runes to write his own private journals and, during the Thirty Years War, a runic code was devised by the Swedes to convey clandestine messages from one army to another during battles. Such use of the ancient runes would have pleased the Norse war god, Tew, and Odin himself!

We hear little of runes from the seventeenth century until the close of the nineteenth, when the first stirrings of German nationalism began to be noticed. There was then a revival of popular interest in ancient beliefs pertaining to the teutonic races, including rune lore. In the 1900s a member of the Prussian Herald's Office named Dr Benhard Koener became a devotee of a strange runic cult organized by Guido Von List, whose book *The Secrets Of The Runes* was a bestseller in occult circles. Von List was eventually forced to flee from his home in Vienna when revelations of the weird magical rites indulged in by members of his secret runic order became public knowledge.

Koener became a founder member in 1912 of the German Order, an anti-Semitic, extreme right-wing occult group dabbling in the seamier side of magic. Candidates for initiation into this group, which has been described by modern commentators as a form of 'Nordic freemasonry', were blindfolded and led to meet a white-robed master of ceremonies wearing a Viking helmet and carrying the sacred 'spear of Wotan' (or Odin). The initiate was informed that he was a member of a superior race and that he was to despise all 'inferior' people, such as Jews, Marxists and blacks.

The leaders of the Order signed documents with runic sigils and one of the first instructions to the entered candidate was the correct use of the rune alphabet. Another member of the secret society, Hermann Pohl, sold copper amulet rings engraved with runic symbols which guarded the owner from injury. These rings were much in demand by the officers of the German Imperial Army when war broke out in 1914.

The Thule Society
Dr Benhard Koener himself embroidered the peculiar theories relating to runes propagated by Von List and even suggested that the beams of medieval houses had a runic significance to German coats of arms, which he believed concealed occult truths hidden in esoteric symbols. One of Koener's associates in the German Order, Baron von Sebottendorff, later launched a magazine called *Runen*, or *The Rune*, devoted to Aryan occultism, rune lore and bitter propaganda attacks on the Jews. He believed the Jews were involved in a world-wide conspiracy to control the Gentile race by monopolizing the centres of finance and banking. One of von Sebottendorff's protégés, Walter Nauhaus, was to found the Thule Society, a study group on Nordic magic which is said to have numbered the young Hitler in its ranks. The anti-Semitic Baron purchased in 1918 an obscure publishing house which was later responsible for printing the magazine *Volkischer*

Beobachter, the official journal of the National Socialist Party.

Other German occultists of the same period were also interested in the revival of runecraft, including Siegfried Kumer who invented a system of Aryan yoga which based its postures on the shape of letters in the runic alphabet. He also believed that meditation on a certain rune could cure sickness at a distance and equated various parts of the human anatomy with healing runes. During the 1920s Kumer founded a magical school devoted to the teaching of rune lore, astrology and pagan beliefs.

It was during the 1920s that Adolf Hitler became interested in runes and the occult and was introduced to the 'lunatic fringe' of German occultism. Hitler became obsessed with the pagan heritage of his past and believed that it was his destiny to lead Germany back to power after the First World War. He was attracted to the Thule Society, by then a powerful force in the mystico-political scene of post-war Germany, and as a member rubbed shoulders with high-ranking army and police officers, judges, civil servants, wealthy businessmen, local politicians, university professors and the cream of the rich Bavarian bourgeoisie. All were dedicated anti-Semitics, politically extreme right-wing and fanatical believers in the alleged supremacy of the German race. These men were to become the ruling élite of the National Socialist Party, founded by Hitler to bring the mad dreams of the German occult movement to reality, and they helped launch the insignificant Austrian corporal as the promised Messiah who would lead his chosen people to the pinacle of power. Few realized then that the fanatic they had supported would eventually light the flame that consumed Germany and left it in ruins.

Swastika Symbol

The ancient magical symbols of Western Europe had a tremendous effect on the mind of the young Hitler. He adopted the swastika, or sun wheel, as the sigil of the new Germany, together with the lightning flash or thunderbolt sacred to Thor. When Hitler adapted the swastika he reversed it from the symbol of the sun to the sign of the dark powers of

Swastika emblems at Hitler's May Day speech in 1939.

Hitler's personal SS bodyguard.

the waning moon and under its sign were commited some of the worst horrors ever seen in the long and cruel history of human life.

At the great pre-war Nazi rallies flags embroidered with the swastika fluttered alongside banners emblazoned with runic symbols. Nordic maidens with blonde pigtails marched under the runic flags as priestesses of the German Reich. Those who waved and saluted with straight arms the swastikas passing by knew nothing of the holocaust to come.

Swastikas were not the only link between the Nazi movement and runes. Heinrich Himmler sponsored research into the history of German runes and when he founded his dreaded Schutzstaffel unit of élite stormtroopers he used the double Sig rune *SS* as the design for their badges, flags and armbands. Himmler was fascinated by the occult, as were other Nazi leaders such as Rudolf Hess, and when Himmler controlled the German Secret Intelligence Service he set up a special top secret department called the Occult Bureau to gather information on runic and other magic, astrology, and the possible uses of psychic powers in espionage work. It is rumoured that a similar organization was also set up by the Allied Intelligence network, although proof of its existence is very difficult to establish from official sources of information.

Since the war the study of runes has declined in popularity and in its waning the runes have lost the sinister aspects which became associated with them through the malefic influence of the Nazis. However, a spate of recent books on Saxon archaeological remains has once more spurred interest in the subject and people are beginning to show curiosity towards runecraft. In a recent issue of an astrological journal there appeared an advertisement from a modern rune caster offering 'runic readings' which proves that the ancient art has not lost its glamour as a method of divination. However, the life and death aspect of rune casting has been lost and today it is generally practised only for amusement.

Despite popular exploitation runes have not completely foresaken their original role as purveyors of occult secrets. In a recent news-sheet, sent out from an address in Southern England by the high priest of a revived witchcraft movement, leaders of witch covens were invited to send for a set of runic codes prepared by a Scottish witch. These codes were recommended for 'confidential intercommunication' between modern witches, pending the adoption of a world-wide, standard runic alphabet.

It would seem that, alongside the present revival of the occult in the West, there will still be a place for runes in the secret alphabets of the aspiring magician or witch.

6.

MEDIEVAL MAGIC ALPHABETS

While the runes held sway in Western Europe, the creation and use of mystical alphabets and secret codes had become a sophisticated art among the Arabs, who were renowned in the early Middle Ages as magicians. The North African Moors had extended their empire by AD 711 to include the Sahara and parts of Southern Europe. In the eighth century an army of seven thousand Berber tribesmen invaded Spain and were to hold it as a Moslem stronghold until 1492. Arab supremacy in Europe was complete.

During the period when Spain was under Moorish rule it became a centre for the study and practice of magic and occultism. Scholars and students from England, France and Germany travelled to sit at the feet of Arab, Christian and Jewish philosophers in Spain, and at Toledo was founded the only university ever established to teach magic and sorcery. In the thirteenth century, the cabbala – or mystical inner teaching of the Judaic religion – was first written down from its original oral sources by a Spanish Rabbi and this philosophy became the foundation stone of medieval occultism. It is also the guiding light of the modern revival of magical practices.

In such an atmosphere it is little wonder that the lore of secret alphabets flourished. In AD 855, the occult scholar Abu Bakir Ahmad was the first to include magical Arab scripts in his treatise *Kitab Shaug Almustsham Pi Manifat Rumaz Al-Oglam* or *The Book Of The Frenzied Devotee To Learn About The Ancient*

Scripts. One alphabet he mentioned is called *Dambudi* or *Davidian* taking its name from King David of Israel whose son, Solomon, is considered by the Arabs to be the greatest magician who ever lived.

Solomon is credited with the founding of freemasonry and it is alleged that the masonic graft developed from magical rites known to the stonemasons who constructed the temple of Jerusalem. Despite these romantic fantasies, it is more probable that speculative freemasonry arose from the secret societies organized by tradesmen's guilds in the Middle Ages and the brotherhood of stonemasons who built the great monuments of Christendom. Certainly the wealth of legends surrounding both David and his magic-making son made the Davidian alphabet a very potent tool in the occult armoury of Arab magicians.

The Arabic mystical alphabet named Davidian after King David of Israel, son of the arch-magician Solomon.

The alphabet was derived from Hebrew letters, used by the Jews with certain subtle changes. Tails were added to some letters and in others parts were missing from their outline. In fact it resembles nothing less than a rather esoteric version of the modern Pitman's shorthand but was regarded with awe by the Arabs who, as a tribute to its alleged occult powers, often referred to it simply as *rihani* or 'magic'.

Another alphabet mentioned by Abu Bair Ahmad survived until the eighteenth century, when it was still used by Algerian sorcerors. It was universally known in the Middle East but had different names in various countries – in Turkey it was *misiti* meaning Egyptian, in Cairo in was *shami* or Syrian and in Damascus it was called *tadmin* or *polymere*.

A third Islamic code can be found in the *Kinb Al Mu'am'ma* or *Book Of Secret Languages* written by the poet Abu Abd Al-Kahil (718-791 AD). He began each line of his secret languages with the words 'In the name of Allah' which added extra potency to the script, For the Moslem name for God was widely believed, both inside and outside Islam, to have special powers and was a sacred word to millions of devoted followers of the prophet Mohammed.

In addition to the Arabic alphabets there were codes originating from Persia, one of which substituted the names of birds for letters. A second one equated characters with the twenty-eight lunar mansions in astrology – the degrees through which the moon passes in a month – and the *dragon tails* or nodes of the moon. The key to the Persian alphabets was the replacing of letters by obscure symbols which were supposed to be unknown to anyone not actively engaged in occult pursuits.

Roger Bacon

The thirteenth century inventor and philosopher Roger Bacon was one of the medieval experts on magical writings and he had strong views on the subject. In his book, *Secret Works Of Art And Magick*, he says 'A man is insane who writes a secret in any way other than one which will conceal it from the vulgar'. He goes on to list seven clandestine codes to accomplish this feat, composed of letters from long dead languages, invented characters, shorthand and magico-mystical sigils.

Bacon was believed by his enemies to possess fantastic powers and, like so many famous or unusual men of the period, he was said to have sold his soul to the devil in exchange for knowledge unavailable to ordinary mortals. He was reported to have made a bronze head which spoke in several languages, until it was dropped by a careless student and shattered into a dozen pieces.

Other medieval magicians followed Bacon's example and invented their own secret scripts. An Italian alchemist named de Bruxella used a secret cipher in the fifteenth century to hide details of his alchemical operations from rival practitioners and inquisitive Catholics. He also made the modest claim of discovering the famous *philosopher's stone* which could transform base lead into sparkling gold in the twinkling of a magic wand.

Alchemy itself had a strange symbology, based on word pictures and signs, to disguise its workings. Sulphur and quicksilver, two of the principal elements in the alchemical process, were illustrated in old documents by the astrological sigils for the sun and moon ☉ ☽. The other metals – such as lead, copper or iron – were shown as symbols which later developed into the signs used in modern astrology to depict the planets. These sigils were universally adopted by magicians, alchemists and astrologers in the Middle Ages as coded symbols of the seven classical planets known to ancient man.

Some occultists claimed to have received magical alphabets through divine or angelic communications from beyond the earthly planes and one of these was the German abbot and wizard Trithemuis (1462-1516). He told his gullible pupils that he had been visited by a spirit form who imparted to him a secret script. This consisted of a 'nonsense language' in which some letters were replaced by gibberish, something like 'Ostuim Thatlia chanistrea pomasiel'. The key was apparently based on Latin.

Trithemuis gathered together his magical alphabets and had them published for general use. Unfortunately the silly fellow, for extra effect, had mixed in fragments of cabbalistic magic, conjurations of good and evil spirits and invocations to the angels. His liberal usage of such forbidden arts upset the Catholic Church and his book was placed on the infamous Vatican 'blacklist' of censored publications. Anyone found reading his book was liable to excommunication and even execution as a heretic.

Cipher disc belonging to Giovanni Porta.

The Enochian Alphabet

One of the most famous cryptographers, Dr John Dee, whose strange discoveries we will examine later, also claimed a divine origin for his *Enochian* magical alphabet. He had quite a lot in common with an Italian occult dabbler, Giovanni Porta, who, in the early sixteenth century, founded a magical fraternity in Naples. Porta, like the German abbot, also clashed with the clerical authorities and on one occasion was called before the Pope to explain his 'necromantic experiments' with the flying ointment used by witches. Despite several hair-raising adventures, which many times brought him close to death, Porta managed to escape the grasp of the Church and even invented a magical cipher disc which could be used to break his own codes.

Alphabets used in medieval magic included the *Theban* or *Honourian* – named after the city of Thebes in ancient Egypt and the renegade Pope Honorious, who was one of many wearers of the Papal crown to have craftily dabbled in the black arts – *Celestial*, *Malachim* and *Passing the River*. All these were mentioned by the nineteenth century occultist Francis Barrett in his book *The Magus* (1801) and have survived today, with the Theban script even being renamed the *witches' alphabet* because of its use by people following the revived pagan cult of witchcraft.

The Alphabet of the Hebrews

Alone among the alphabets used for esoteric purposes is one that at first glance would seem to be an unlikely choice, until one delves into its history and long association with things magical. It is, of course, the alphabet of the Hebrews. This system of writing received a wide prominence in the Middle Ages because it was the language of the original books making up the Judeo-Christian Bible and in those times the Old Testament was still regarded as the actual words of God.

According to the cabbalistic treatise *Sepher Yetzirah* or *Book Of Creation* everything came into being when God spoke the twenty-two letters of the Hebrew alphabet. This was the esoteric meaning behind the words 'God said, "Let there be light" and there was light' since, because the word was spoken in Hebrew, it must be the language of creation. By evoking the powers hidden in its letters a brave magician could control all living creatures and be able to create at will, becoming one with God. In an earlier chapter we saw how Enoch was given the magical letters by the archangel Metraton and we are safe in assuming that these letters were the twenty-two letters of the Hebrew alphabet.

When the gypsies brought the magical set of playing cards called the *tarot* or *tarochi* to Europe from the Near East in the fourteenth century, Hebrew scholars recognized in the twenty-two cards of the *major arcana* the letters of the Hebrew alphabet.

The twenty-two letters, or keys, of the Hebrew alphabet were divided into three separate groups having rulership over various spheres of the material plane. Twelve were assigned to the signs of the zodiac, the months of the year, the major organs of the human body and the twelve senses and emotions. Seven were given to the classical planets known in ancient times (i.e. sun, moon, Venus, Mars, Jupiter and Saturn), the days of the week and the directions of the compass.

Finally, the three remaining letters of *Mem-Shin-Aleph*, sometimes referred to as the 'mother' letters, were given to the three elements of fire, earth and water, the three seasons of the old calendar (spring, summer, winter), to earth, heaven and hell, and finally to the three divisions of the body – head, abdomen and legs.

Naturally, the three prime mother letters were considered the most powerful in the alphabet and the others were reserved for minor acts of magic. The Hebrew letters were regarded as doubly potent because of the numerical value of each character which meant that the name of a person, animal or place could be broken down into the *master numbers* of 1-9, each having a special meaning.

Hebrew letters were also juggled to form the secret names of God and the medieval magician believed that he could summon up elemental spirits and demons by calling out these names during his rites of conjuration. The names were coded versions of the various titles given to the Hebrew God, the best known being the holy name of the tetragrammaton (i.e. four words) or *Yod He Wau He*. This was written in simplified form as YHWH and means 'I am who I am' revealing the fundamental truth that if God thinks then He exists. YHWH is the esoteric version of the God name Jehovah, which was used in the Middle Ages by magicians to call up-spirits and summon angels.

Another word regarded as even more powerful than the tetragrammaton was the 'word of twenty-two letters', for its sacred number not only had a connection with the Hebrew alphabet but also with the number of key cards in the tarot. This secret word can be found in *The Book Of The Angel Batziel*, first published in thirteenth century Germany, and is written thus: ANTQM PSTM POPYM DYVNSYM. Many alternative translations of this sacred word have been made but the general agreement among Hebrew scholars is that it is a code based on the traditional blessing given by the Rabbi '... and the Lord keep ye and bless ye, the Lord make His face to shine upon ye, the Lord lift up his countenance and give ye peace everlasting.'

There is also rumoured to be a forty-two letter word considered potent to bind troublesome demons. A fifteenth-century magus, John de Rayne, was said to have called up the demon Samuetz (not to be confused with the archangel Samuel), the husband of the goddess Lilith, and bound him by placing on his head a crown engraved with the forty-two letters of the prime magical word. As in all good fairy tales for adults, the demon cheated the magician and de Rayne lived miserably ever after. Let that be a warning to those who think calling up demons is fun.

The importance of Hebrew as a powerful magical alphabet has survived to the present day. That renowned bisexual magician Aleister Edward Crowley (1875-1947) once lamented that, when he applied to join the Hermetic Order Of The Golden Dawn in 1898, he was bound by terrible oaths which threatened instant death if he ever betrayed the arcane secrets of the Order. Once he had entered the group all he was taught was the Hebrew alphabet and, in his youthful folly, the young Crowley did not regard this as a secret worthy of

Medieval Magical alphabets.

keeping under pain of unpleasant death. No doubt he changed his mind in later years, when he realized the occult knowledge concealed in the Hebrew letters.

7.

THE ENOCHIAN SCRIPT

During the reign of Queen Elizabeth I, an astrologer and mathematician by the name of Dr John Dee (1527-1608) discovered a magical alphabet which, though still little understood by occultists, is both feared and respected by them for its power to unleash the most fantastic elemental forces.

Dee called his system the *Enochian calls* or *keys*, naming them after the prophet Enoch who 'walked with God and was not'. The Enochian alphabet was received by Dee through his medium, Edward Kelly (aka Tabot), who gazed into a crystal or *shewstone* owned by his astrologer master and divined the symbols perceived in its misty depths.

Edward Kelly was a man shrouded in mystery and controversy. His claim to fame before meeting the good doctor was for losing his ears for dabbling in necromancy and he habitually wore a black skull cap pulled down to hide his deformity. The act of necromancy in which he had been caught red-handed was a rite, performed with his accomplice Paul Waring at night in a Lancashire churchyard, to invoke the dead. The two rogues had dug up a corpse and by magical incantations were trying to cajole it to predict the future. A romantic woodcut of the two sorcerors at their grisly game can be found in *The Astrologer Of The Nineteenth Century* and certain sensational modern writers have identified the two men depicted as Kelly and Dee. In fact, this happened before they met.

Dr Dee was the opposite of his assistant. He was an

authority on astronomy, navigation and optics, an accomplished graduate from St John's College, Cambridge, Royal astrologer to both Queen Mary and Queen Elizabeth and a well-travelled student of international politics. During his many visits to Europe, including several years studying at the University of Louvain, he met with famous occultists such as Cornelius Agrippa, author of *The Philosophy Of Magic*, who

Dr John Dee

instructed the English scientist in the magical arts.

In 1563 Dee read, with great excitement, the book *Stenographia*, by our old friend Trimethuis, which gave details of magical alphabets, ciphers and codes, as well as demonic magic. Dee became fascinated by both subjects and, when he returned to England, he took up crystal gazing in an attempt to contact the spirits described by Trimethuis as the authors of magical alphabets.

The crystal and waxen tablets used by Dee and Kelly were purchased by the British Museum at a Sotheby's auction in 1942 and now reside in that great hall of post culture, along with Dee's original manuscripts and a gold disc allegedly cast from base metal by the use of the philosopher's stone. The latter had been picked up by the two magicians on one of their trips to the ruined abbey at Glastonbury in Somerset.

Each word of the Enochian alphabet, which Dee claimed to have received from an extraterrestrial source, was given letter by letter and backwards. The reason for this was that the spirit transmitting the alphabet advised Dee that the magical forces behind its letters were so powerful that, even during dictation, if the letters were given in their correct order they could be let loose and cause indescribable havoc. Each word represented a previously unknown name of God, his angels and the elemental spirits and Dee copied down the words using a special cipher to further hide their meaning from the uninitiated.

The Four Castles

He later evolved this cipher into five Enochian squares, or tablets. Four of these symbolized the material elements of fire, earth, air and water. Table number five was assigned to *aeythr*, or spirit, the hidden element regarded by occultists as the permeating cosmic energy of the created (and uncreated) universe. Having received the tablets, Kelly was then given the so-called 'vision of the ground plan of the universe or Enochian cosmos' or the 'vision of the four castles'. A representation of this magical blueprint of creation is engraved on the golden disc preserved in the horological gallery of the British Museum.

The four castles correspond to Celtic myths of the 'castles of the four winds' guarded by the goddess Arianhod, whose name means the silver wheel and refers to the Milky Way constellation in the night sky. In fact the strange world of Dee's Enochia resembles quite closely the elemental kingdoms of the Celtic legends described in fairy tales and myths. The four castles can also be seen as symbols of the four quarters of the magician's circle, ruled by the Hebrew archangels, Mikael, Raphael, Gabriel and Uriel, and the four 'watchtowers' of north, south, east and west surrounding the nine foot circles of modern witchcraft covens. These are traditionally governed by the 'mighty ones' regarded by some witches as departed ancestors now elevated to semi-divine status, aspects of the horned god and the moon goddess or as the four kings of the elemental worlds.

Each Enochian Castle was associated with a different hue of the spectrum. Red (east), white (south), green (west) and black (north). These colours seem to be a variation on the elementary colours of red or orange (fire), yellow or white (air), blue and silver (water) and brown or green (earth). The four castles in Celtic lore do have a seasonal significance – north is winter, south is summer, east is spring and west is autumn. Taking all these facts into consideration we can presume that the four castles or watchtowers are symbols of the boundaries of the Enochian universe, an alternative cosmos which can be entered through the keys provided by the words of the Enochian alphabet.

In practical terms there are thirty aethyrs or calls in the alphabet. These consist of groups of letters such as OXO, LIT, MAZ, TOR, NIA, ZAA, LEA, DES, ZAK etc., seeming at first glance to be the remains of some long-lost ancient language. Occultists believe that this is what Enochian might be, the remnants of the alphabet and language written and spoken by the priest-magicians of the lost land of Atlantis. If this is so, and I might add here that there is not the slightest shred of evidence to support such a speculative claim, then the Enochian alphabet is revealed as the oldest magical code in existence, for the destruction of Atlantis is theoretically dated many tens of thousands of years before the first dynasties of

Ancient Egypt. Interesting as such a hypothesis is, it will remain only that until archaeological research either proves or disproves the reality of Atlantis.

Language experts who have examined the Enochian alphabet dismiss completely the theories linking it to the Atlantean past. Richard Deacon, a modern biographer of Dr Dee, has even gone one step better and alleged that the complete system was the invention of Dee. He states that the alphabet is a very sophisticated code used by the astrologer while engaged on spying missions for Francis Walsingham, the founder of the British Secret Service. According to this very plausible theory, Dee utilized his cover as an eccentric occultist to gain the interest of European noblemen and royalty and then spied upon them, sending back coded information to London in messages written in the 'language of the angels'.

The Enochian alphabet, received from an angel by the sixteenth century astrologer and mathematician, John Dee.

Astral Keys

Whether this is true or not, occultists still claim that the Enochian calls are keys for unlocking the astral gateways to another dimension beyond the normal limitations of time and space. If misused in any way the elemental tablets can release powers of great destruction, which will operate through the element represented by any one tablet. Tales have been told of mysterious fires breaking out, water pipes bursting or floorboards caving in as a result of dabbling in Enochian magic. Since people who are actively engaged in occult practices tend to be by nature a romantic crowd, such stories could be exaggerated. But there is a grain of truth in the comment made to the author by one experienced ritual magician who warned, 'Playing around with Enochian magic is like playing around with nuclear fission and one should not be too surprised if there are explosive results'.

Providing the apprentice magician does not blow himself to astral pieces, what kind of world can he gain access to through the careful evocation of the Enochian words of power? The following comments were made in an occult magazine some years ago and they describe the experiences a student of Dee's occult system can expect once the forces of Enochia have been evoked.

(He) will see the beautiful colours within these (Enochian) names, feel the forces that emanate from them and be transported to a strange world long since passed from this earth. He will walk the great plains and mountains of a strange, ancient kingdom across which pass red-eyed horses bearing strange gods in glowing robes of pure colour. He will see the sun rise from dark mountains into a sky of violet and gold.

It would seem that not only could a magician enter the astral worlds of the Enochian plane but entities from that alternative existence could materialize in our time-Space continuum. At one stage spirits actually stepped from Dee's crystal and conversed with the astounded doctor and Kelly in English but with a 'strange accent'. One of the spirit people walked around the room, asking the doctor which monarch sat upon the throne and conversing on subjects connected with everyday life in Tudor times.

The Enochian alphabet is therefore unique in two ways. Firstly, it promises contact between the physical world of men and the domain of spirits, while most other magical alphabets can only conceal knowledge and hide secrets. Secondly, it is not based on alien symbols of characters but uses the ordinary Latin alphabet jumbled up to form new words.

The following extract from the calls illustrates this fact.

'Coraxo chis cormp od blans wcal aziazor lucal aziazor poeb ilonan chis op virg eophan od radir maasi bagle coasgi ds ialpan dosig od basgim od orex claziz siatris od salbrox cinxir faboan unal chis const ds doax cocasg ol oanito yorb votuim gizyak od matb cocasg plosi molvi ds page ip brag om droln matorb cocasb emna L patraix yoki matb nomig manons oharo enay angelard ohio ohio ohio ohio noib ohio coasgon bagle madrid i zir od chiso drilpa nilso crip ip nidali.'

Translated, as far as it is possible, into English this reads:

> The thunders of judgement and wrath are numbered and are harboured in the north in the likeness of an oak whose branches are nests of lamentations and weepings, laid up for the Earth, which burn night and day and vomit out the heads of scorpions and live sulphur mixed with poison. These be the thunders that five thousand six hundred and seventy-eight times in ye twenty-fourth part of a moment roar with a hundred mighty earthquakes and a thousand times surge, which rest not neither know any echoing time therein. One rock bringeth forth thousands even as the heart of man doth his thoughts. Woe! Woe! Woe! Woe! Be to the Earth for her iniquity is, was and shall be great. Come away, but not ye mighty sounds.

If this resembles any known language the closest would be Spanish, or the ancient Aztec tongue spoken in Mexico and South America. Occult traditions, which are seldom accurate, point to both Spain and South America as colonies established by the survivors of Atlantis. The theory is postulated that Dr Dee and Edward Kelly were in mediumistic contact with the spirit of an Atlantean high priest or priestess who dictated to them the lost language and magical knowledge once taught in the temples of Atlantis.

Interestingly enough, Dee regarded some aethyrs as actual places under or on the earth's surface and he even described the twentieth aethyr as taking up a position under the south pole and inhabited by little men with long beards (Gnomes?). He also describes one of the places of the calls as the site of Atlantis, as described by Plato in his famous *Republic*.

Meric Causabon

An account of Dee's investigations of Enochia were published in *A True And Faithfull Relation Of What Passed Between Dr John Dee And Some Spirits* written by Meric Causabon in 1659. This book was based on Dee's magical diary and until recently was only available for study in the Reading Room at the British Museum. It has now been reprinted by a London publisher specializing in rare occult works and is more readily available to the discerning student of Enochian magic.

Causabon was openly sceptical on occult matters and described Dee as a 'deluded charlatan searching for dreams'. It was this damning rejection of Dee that gave him such a bad name in academic circles. For many years his achievements were ridiculed by the scientific establishment and his breakthroughs in the realm of navigation and astronomy were ignored or dismissed as charlatanism. His opponents were more interested in condemning Dee as a 'black magician' then praising his outstanding work for the advancement of early scientific knowledge.

Modern magicians, using Causabon's book as a source, have expanded the Enochian alphabet as a magical system per se within the framework of practical occult techniques. The groundwork for these adapations was laid out in the Hermetic Order Of The Golden Dawn by such people as Samuel (McGregor) Mathers and Aleister Crowley, both leading personalities in the Order and translators of the old texts or *grimoires* on medieval magic. The version of the Enochian system practised by these two magi can be found in Dr Israel Regardie's monumental two volume work, *The Rites And Teachings Of The Golden Dawn*, originally published in 1940 but now reissued by an occult publishing house.

In the GD system, the tarot is linked with the elemental tablets together with cabbalistic attributions. The various stages of psychic development in the system of dimensional communication are aligned with the grades of magical profiency within the Order. Occultists love to complicate even the most simple thing and in the GDs interpretation of Enochia (which is complicated enough without any further additions) we have a classic example of this process in action.

Enochian Chess
The members of the GD also invented a game based on Dr Dee's magic, called Enochian or Rosicrucian chess, and this

was taught and played by the higher grades in the fraternity. Enochian chess used four boards – based on the elemental tablets – and the pieces were in the shape of Ancient Egyptian gods. The squares on the boards were painted in the elemental colours and were so arranged that when placed next to each other they seemed to 'flash'. Each board represented one of the watchtowers of the elements and, as well as its use as a game, Enochian chess was also used for divination. When divining, the elemental boards were seen in reference to the tarot and the elements of fire, earth, air and water were defined as the four suits of the *minor arcana* – swords (or wands), pentacles, wands (or swords) and cups.

In Enochian chess the pawns of modern chess were the four sons of Horus or the Canopic gods, so-called because their image appeared on the jars containing the viscera of the deceased. Their attributions were as follows.

Fire Kabexnuv – the mummy-shaped god with a hawk's head.

Earth Ameshet – the mummy-shaped god with a human face.

Air Ahephi – the mummy-shaped god with a monkey's head.

Water Tmoumathph – the mummy-shaped god with dog or jackal's head.

The major pieces of the game not only resembled Egyptian gods but were also symbols of the court cards in the tarot, the kings, queens, knights etc. of swords, pentacles, wands and cups. So complicated were the rules for playing Enochian chess that the instructions on how to set up and complete a game cover some twenty pages in the 'knowledge papers' of the Order.

So complex was the subject of Enochian magic in the GD that one of its members, disguised by the title Frater A.M.A.G., claimed to possess manuscripts totalling seventy thousand words, together with dozens of large charts, coloured illustrations and boards handed down from the original founders of the Order who were believed to be high-ranking German Rosicrucians and freemasons.

Another GD member, Frater D.D.C.F., claimed: 'The tablets of Enoch require many years of study and will repay such an expenditure of time and energy. The knowledge embodied in these manuscripts (the knowledge papers) is very superficial and elementary and entirely fails to do justice to the Enochian scheme. You (the student) must take it as only a feeble attempt to provide what is seen at first glance, by the intellect and as having no relation to the world of spiritual truth which the tablets enshrine and which a high Adept can make them give out.'

Before a Golden Dawn student could attempt to master the Enochian alphabet he was first tested on his theoretical and practical knowledge of magic. He had to prove that he knew the meanings, both esoteric and exoteric, of the tarot cards, that he was skilled in geomantic divination, could recite the Hebrew alphabet and be aware of its occult powers and mysteries, was knowledgeable on the cabbala and the symbols of the tree of life. Further to this he was expected to memorize and be proficient in the pentagram and hexagram rituals, the formulae of the consecration rite, and be able to draw talismanic sigils with skill. If he could prove his worth in all these tests then, and only then, did the officers of the Order regard him as properly prepared to handle the powerful forces of Enochia.

When Regardie issued the details of the Golden Dawn Enochian system he too gave a warning to the curious and the dilettante. '(Enochian) is a very powerful system and if carelessly used will bring about disaster and spiritual disintegration. The warnings given about the invocations are not to be regarded as platitudinous moralizing but represent knowledge of the true facts. Let the student study the tablets first, so that they are ingrained in his mind. Only when that has been accomplished can he dare to use the invocations in ceremonial.'

When one hears modern occultists boasting of their work with the Enochian system these wise words come to mind and are a warning to those who would experiment with this powerful and terrible magical alphabet.

8.

ALPHABET OF DESIRE

Three hundred years separate the Elizabethan magus, Dr
John Dee, from the artist and mystic Austin Osman Spare
(1888-1956), yet both men shared a terrifying contact with
other levels of reality and both were responsible for unique
magical alphabets allegedly derived from otherworldly
sources.

Spare was driven even more than his sixteenth-century
counterpart by the creative urge. By the age of twenty he had
written books outlining his strange theories and had held a
private exhibition of drawings, pastels and paintings
illustrating the nightmare world that he believed existed just
outside the normal range of human senses. His inspiration for
these trips into the dark otherworld of the subconscious was
an old lady who claimed to be an initiate of the traditional
witch cult and it was she was instructed him in the ancient
ways of forgotten magic. Spare often told of her psychic ability
to conjure up thought forms so vividly that they actually
materialized and could be seen by other people.

The young artist was taught the technique of thought
visualization by the old witch and this teaching stimulated
him to evoke, with pen and pencil, the weird denizens of the
elemental kingdoms and the grotesque attendants of the
witches' sabbath. Strange creatures, half-human and half-
satyr, writhe across the pages of his drawing book. Odd,
elemental faces peer from the tortured trunks of aged trees.

Demons and humanoid devils dance in mocking abandonment with old hags at some grand nocturnal celebration. Ancient crones are suddenly transformed to beautiful sirens as the glamour of witchcraft blurs the edges of everyday reality.

Many of these drawings and paintings had an explicit sexual content and this aspect of Spare's artistic work offended many of the strait-laced art critics and gallery owners of the time. West End galleries refused to stage any of Spare's exhibitions or hang his paintings, and even fellow artists, renowned for their Bohemian views, shunned the young artist as if he was guilty of some terrible crime against humanity.

Spare was a person who despised convention and the Establishment, so this treatment by the art world had little effect on him. He decided that if they wanted none of him then he had no desire to continue as part of their closed and restricted world. He elected to follow a solitary path of artistic creativity and vanished from the art scene into the slums of South London, where he became just one more faceless inhabitant of the teeming metropolis.

In his new environment Spare led a precarious existence, drawing portraits of local characters and selling them for a few pounds in public houses. While this kept the rent up to date, he was privately engaged in his true work on the magical path and was on the brink of discovering a magic alphabet based upon ancient atavistic symbols. This alphabet, was, in its own way, as significant as the Enochian system discovered by Dee and Kelly in their mystical experiments with the crystal.

At one stage in his career Spare had been a member of an occult group organized by Aleister Crowley and the 'great beast' had exerted a tremendous influence on the developing psyche of the magus and artist. Spare was in agreement with Crowley that sex was fundamental to any really potent form of magical working and in his first major book, *The Focus Of Life*, he says, 'there is only one sense and that is sexual'. Like Crowley, he associated with street women and neurotics but any pleasure he received from these encounters was channelled into magical rites. He used his female associates as

Aleister Crowley, the 'Great Beast'   Austin Osman Spare

instruments to communicate with the spirit world. He regarded them as *succubae*, or female demons, and is recorded as boasting that he could sleep with six or seven women in one night without losing vitality.

Spare eventually disagreed with Crowley, as did most people after a while, and left him to pursue his studies on independent lines of research. It was during this period that he began to formulate his own magical alphabet and to create a system which is now regarded as his greatest contribution to practical occultism. The alphabet was lost to public sight after Austin Spare's death in 1956, although it was known to a few of his close friends and magical associates. Recently, however, several of his works, originally privately printed, have been published and there is renewed interest in the alphabet's occult symbolism and practical uses.

Austin Spare called his system of magical working *the alphabet of desire* and based it upon individual symbols which he said had arisen from his own subconscious mind. These sigils were either composed of interlaced letters signifying the first letters of a phrase such as 'I wish to be rich' – the key letters IWTBR being used to form a symbol – or an abstract symbol representing either a psychic force or some desire of the magician translated through the association of ideas.

Atavistic Resurgence

He even made a pack of cards painted with the symbols of the new alphabet and carried them in his pocket at all times. Spare's theory was that the magician could visualize and concentrate on the card symbol and this would awaken the corresponding powers in his subconscious, attracting his desire (e.g. wealth, women or power) to him. This technique of positive thinking he called *atavistic resurgence* and he claimed that, once the desire image had been evoked, providing the magician was adept in the art, it could be externalized as either a projected thought form or an idea impregnated in the mind of a receptive receiver.

This was the theory behind the technique but there were many examples of the practical demonstration of the process. One anecdote relates that Spare was challenged to produce rain by magical means. As the day was sunny and hot, with a clear blue sky, it seemed as if the task was an impossible one. Undaunted, Spare wrote one of his alphabetic symbols on a scrap of paper and concentrated on it with the whole force of his will-power.

Within a few minutes clouds began to mass above Spare and his companion and in a short while it began to rain. The torrent turned to a deluge and both men were soaked to the skin. The magician's theories had been vindicated in practice.

Other experiments with magic had more unpleasant results. One day two dabblers in the occult turned up on Spare's doorstep and insisted that the artist conjured up an elemental spirit for them. At first he refused but they were so adamant in their desire to see such an entity that eventually he conceded their wish. Spare used one of his sigils to evoke the spirit and after a few minutes the dingy room began to fill with greenish mist. A pungent fishy smell was noticed by the two visitors and they watched paralyzed as a demonic face began to form in the green cloud. Weird eyes, like pinpoints of fire, glowed from slanted slits and the terrified 'occultists' began to scream to Spare to banish the evoked elemental. Eventually he did banish the entity and it vanished as quickly as it had arrived, leaving only the lingering stench of rotten fish to mark its passing.

Within a few days of this rite one of Spare's two visitors died under mysterious circumstances and the other witness eventually ended up in a mental hospital under sedation. Spare was unrepentant, for he regarded the experience as a lesson to amateurs who try to call upon forces which they little understand and cannot control once evoked.

Austin Spare, like his teacher Crowley, believed that good results could be obtained in magical operations by exhausting the body to the point where the mind became completely detached from everyday cares and worries. Once forged, such a mental instrument was capable of achieving magical results quickly and without undue effort.

Such states of physical exhaustion coupled with mental alertness could be gained in a variety of ways. Fasting, gymnastic exercises, lack of sleep or strenuous sexual activity were all methods used by magicians such as Spare and Crowley, either singly or in a series of combinations. When the body attained the desired level of exhaustion the mind was then at its most lucid and the individual's imagined abstract desires could. be conjured into concrete existence by concentrated meditation on the atavistic alphabet.

In his attempts to obtain results in this way Spare often spent several days and nights without sleep or food and engaged in sexual acts with many different women. By this process he came to a state of readiness enabling him to function on many different levels of magical action – physical, mental and psychic.

Sidetracking the Conscious Mind

Although, the leading requirement of magic is concentration, Spare believed that if a magician tried too hard to achieve something the strength of his will would negate the effort and by natural law the desired object would remain outside his grasp. At the actual moment of evocation Spare insisted that the desire should be erased from the mind of the magician. The principle operating behind magic was to side-track the conscious mind and commune directly with the subconscious, which did not understand words but could be reached through the medium of symbolic images.

If the conscious mind was aware of the results required, a mental block was created and the spell would come to a negated conclusion. Only by disassociating one level from another could the occultist allow the magical force called up by the atavistic alphabet to find a free channel of expression. Then the goal of the operation could be realized and the person would obtain the desired results.

The magic of Austin Osman Spare was associated with the goddess of the old pagan religion and to the artist she was the ultimate representation of atavistic resurgence. In his art he depicted the goddess in the form of Astarte, Isis and other Eygptian deities but he also regarded any limitation of the goddess in a physical form as destructive to the flow of magical power. He condemned magicians, such as the Golden Dawn people, who donned ritual disguises to represent the old gods because he believed that man was already an aspect of the godhead and needed no mask or mummery to emphasize the fact.

In the latter years of his life Spare began to mix with fellow wayfarers on the occult path and made a few extra pounds by supplying talismans and amulets to other practitioners of the art. Kenneth Grant, who knew Spare during that last period of his life, tells the story of one of these talismans in the occult encyclopedia *Man, Myth And Magic* and relates the tragic circumstances which followed its making.

A witch joined Grant's magical group, but the high priest of her parent coven consulted Austin Spare in an attempt to get her back to the fold. According to Kenneth Grant, the artist was in total ignorance of the matter and had been merely asked to provide a talisman to 'restore that which has been stolen to its rightful place'. As commissioned, Spare made the correct talisman, using sigils from his magical alphabet to bind the spell. When he had completed the object it was passed to the witch-priest.

A few days later a ritual was held at the new group's address and in it the renegade witch was called upon to lay on the altar in a trance. The object of the ceremony was to invoke the goddess Isis to speak through the recumbent priestess. As it happened the ceremony came to a totally different conclusion.

In the middle of the invocation to the Egyptian deity the girl on the altar suddenly sat upright, eyes staring and skin glistening with sweat. A cold wind swept through the room and afterwards the priestess told the others present that she had seen a monstrous bird-like creature fly in through the window. It seemed to seize her in its claws, carry her out into the dark streets and over the snow-covered rooftops. Eventually the bird returned her to the room and she fell from its talons back onto the black-draped altar.

Examination of the window showed that on one of the frost covered panes was etched the unmistakable print of a large bird's claw. On the windowsill was a lump of gelatinous slime which dissolved leaving a strong odour of sea water. Shortly afterwards, Kenneth Grant reveals, the girl emigrated to New Zealand but was drowned en voyage when her ship sank in a storm.

Grant contacted Austin Spare and asked him whether he had been commissioned by the rival priest to make a talisman and, if so, had he bound an elemental spirit into the object, as was often his practice. The artist replied that he had been approached and told Grant that he had conjured up a spirit to inhabit the talisman. When pressed for a description, Spare replied, 'It was a sort of amphibious owl with bat wings and the talons of an eagle'. An almost identical description of the strange creature which had attacked the girl during the rite to Isis.

'Black' Magic
Incidents like these affirm the belief of many moderns that Spare's magic was of the 'black' type and he tends to be labelled as a practitioner of the *lefthand-path*. This term covers such diverse subjects as the evocation of demonic spirits, Satanism and the calling up of the dead. If we take these practices as the criteria for examining Austin Spare's work we find that he is innocent of all charges of taking part in such

morbid arts. Although he was often described as a 'Satanic occultist', there is no evidence of conscious diabolism on his part and, like his guru Crowley, his belief in the devil – if it existed at all – was in the nature of a two-fingered gesture at conventional society and its hypocritical morality.

Spare's magical alphabet has yet to be properly analyzed or evaluated as a separate system of magic and any interest in the man and his work is largely due to the efforts of his literary executor, Kenneth Grant, who is the author of a biography of the strange artist. It is accepted, though, that Spare was a gifted craftsman with pen and paint brush and a recent exhibition of his work at a Chelsea gallery attracted much praise from the critics.

Spare often claimed that many of his paintings were executed while his conscious self was entranced and that otherworld entities worked through him, using his hands to paint while he was unconscious of their actions. He came to know and recognize one of the principal spirits that worked through him, giving him the name Black Eagle and seeing him as a North American Indian. Spare regarded this spirit in the same way as Spiritualist mediums do their guides, although his entity was more like a familiar spirit. In fact, Spare was accepted by the Spiritualists as a *psychic artist* and, when his exhibition was held at the Tamarind Gallery, a reporter from the *Psychic News* was sent along to review the paintings for its readership. Austin Spare had achieved conventional fame at last and, wherever he was then, he must have cringed with embarrassed indignation.

If Spare's own analysis of the source of his artistic gift was correct, then he was a trully remarkable psychic worthy of close study. He was a fitting candidate to adopt the mantle of other great magical cryptographers of the past, such as Roger Bacon, Dr John Dee and the rune masters of the Nordic Age.

9.
THE SIGN OF THOTH

Writing was easily the most important early discovery by mankind, excluding the wheel and fire. Today, we accept it as a matter of course and only express surprise when we are informed that some million people in Britain, despite modern educational methods (or perhaps because of them), cannot read or write.

It is true that humanity survived as an illiterate species for many thousands of years before the creation of writing but, once the revelation of linking symbols together to create words occurred, early civilization was enriched and invigorated by the new semantic art. Man was now in a position to communicate his ideas to others in a lasting form, more durable then the speculated telepathic communication which was perhaps practised in earlier times.

We can have little idea of the initial impact of writing on daily life, for it must have caused many socio-political changes as the established priesthood or government (the elders of the tribe or Royal family of a country) saw the great power that writing had given in to their hands to serve them. Today the shelves of our bookcases overflow with written data, a press of a button puts us in instant visual touch with nearly every part of the world and our lives are influenced, disturbed, ennobled and sometimes even controlled by the vast outflow of printed words directed at us from every side. Remembering the belief of early man that writing and alphabets were divine gifts from the gods, we might be forgiven for thinking that, if this were so, they were a gift from satan not gods.

The emphasis in the modern world is away from written words, whether scratched by pen on paper or hammered out on a typewriter, and towards technologically advanced forms of communication. Video systems are becoming the communicators of the future and we are returning full circle to the picture symbols of the Ancient Egyptians, as visual communication replaces written alphabets. In use the video system is like a visual tape recorder with both sound and vision recorded on magnetic tapes and played back on a cassette. Linked up to a computer, it can produce instant pictures or films from the computerized memory bank at the flick of a switch.

To our ancient ancestors such a machine would have been regarded as magic and the picture glyphs flashing on to the video screen would have been the ultimate magical alphabet. This brings us rather neatly to the question, 'Do we really have a need in modern society for a magical alphabet per se?'

Religion in the twentieth century has ceased to need a special alphabet to conceal secrets from the masses. It would be nonsensical in a religion where there are no secrets to hide. However, when the believer – whether he or she be Christian, Buddhist, Moslem, Jew or Hindu – begins to question the teachings of his religion and to seek truth elsewhere, he enters a secretive realm, where often deception and delusion masquerade as truth. In this strange country the guideposts are often written in clandestine scripts. The doubter seeks in this land the mysteries concealed within the outer kernel of orthodox religion, and entry to the occult or hidden mysteries usually means a password in some magical alphabet.

Today it is often the religious 'heretic' who has recourse to the alphabets of magic, and the ones used come directly from the medieval and classical examples examined earlier in this book. Secret languages, such as Enochian, are traditionally the province of occult societies, but not exclusively so, for many other ethnic and social groups can claim secret methods of communication which assist the preservation of their identity among strangers.

Criminals, American truck drivers, show business people, Cockneys – all have their unique vocabularies so that they can communicate without others understanding what they are talking about. One of the oldest forms of these 'secret' languages is preserved in the counting system employed by sherpherds in Lincolnshire. It runs as follows.

Yan, tan, thethera, pethera, pimp, sethera, lethera, hovera, covera, dik, yan-a-dik, tan-a-dik, tethera-a-dik, pethera-a-dik, bumpit, yan-a-bumpit, tan-a-bumpit, tethera bumpit, pethera bumpit, figgit.

In Sussex there was a different shepherd's language and the counting was as follows.

One-erum, two-erum, cock-erum, shu-erum, seth-erum, shath-erum, winberry, wagtail, tarry diddle, don.

Romany Language

The gypsy travelling people also had their secret Romany language, although few know it today. True Romany gypsies have been replaced by the *didikais*, or half-breeds, and the Irish tinkers, so it is difficult to discern what magical alphabets the travelling folk might have had originally. The gypsy tribes came from India some thousand years ago and English has taken from the old Romany tongue such words as 'pal', from the gypsy *phral* meaning brother, and 'cosh' from *krash*, or a fighting stick.

Apart from Romany, the gypsies employed a secret code known as *patrin*, which was a form of sign writing used to warn their fellows of trouble and to communicate between clans. Signs were left on gateposts, tree trunks and walls, or consisted of two crossed sticks, a pile of stones or a sigil drawn in the dust. For example, two bent sticks signified people on foot, branched twigs indicated a family with young ones and straight sticks meant people in a motor car.

In many cases the meanings of the signs differed from tribe to tribe and even from family to family. While there may have been a common code for all gypsies, individuals and families often adapted this for their own use.

What is the future for magical alphabets and languages?

The revival of interest in occultism and magic which has characterized the 1960s and 70s has naturally seen a revived acceptance of secret codes and ciphers. Modern magicians, like their ancient counterparts, are romantics – they need secrecy to cloak their activities, as a fish needs water to swim in. I quote the words of the nineteenth century magus, Eliphas Lévi: 'To know – to will – to dare – to keep secret!' The last of these was important for it was believed that if magical rites were common knowledge the occult power inherent in them would be lost.

When the modern practitioner of the arcane sciences writes a ritual or a spell in his working book and uses a secret code he or she has several very good reasons for taking this course of action. First, it is concealing the meaning of what has been written from the outsider who could discover the spell and, therefore, by magical logic, dissipate the power. Obviously, unless the writer uses an alphabet of his own creation, it is not going to conceal anything from fellow magicians.

Another reason for the magi having an occult alphabet is that it assists concentration and stops the mind wandering from the chosen goal. If the practitioner has to concentrate on copying an obscure and difficult script, the mind will remain fixed on that objective and there will be little temptation to wander abroad. When the writer was receiving training, his teacher would have impressed on him that the use of magic alphabets in drawing the occult squares of the art was essential. Only by concentration can magic work, and the greater the concentration the more successful the results of the work. Without personal effort no results will be achieved. The magical alphabet is an important item in the magician's armoury and an essential aid to the correct application of occult forces.

BIBLIOGRAPHY

Barratt, Francis *The Magus* (London 1801)

Causabon, Meric *A True And Faithful Account Of What Passed Between Dr John Dee And Some Spirits* (Originally printed 1659, published by Askins 1975)

Cavendish, Richard *Man, Myth And Magic*

Dee, Dr John *Monas Hieroglyphica* (Watkins 1962)

Elliott, Prof. R. *Runes* (Manchester University Press 1963)

Glob, Prof. P.V. *The Mound People* (Faber & Faber 1974)

Grant, Kenneth *The Magical Revival* (Frederick Muller 1973)

Graves, Robert *The White Goddess* (Faber & Faber 1948)

King, Francis *Satan And Swastika* (Mayflower 1976)

Ravenscroft, Trevor *The Spear Of Destiny* (Neville Spearman 1972)

Regardie, Dr F. Israel *The Golden Dawn* (Llewellyn Publications)

Simpson, J. *Everyday Life In Viking Times* (Batsford 1970)